D1137042

hampsteadtheatre and
Liverpool Everyman and Playhouse present

3 sisters on hope street

by Diane Samuels and Tracy-Ann Oberman, after Anton Chekhov

Production Sponsor

Bank Leumi (UK) plc

Commission supported by

European Association
for Jewish Culture

Media Sponsor

JEWISH NEWS
& MEDIA GROUP
SIMCHAS *Pulse*

A&B
Arts & Business *working together*

Corporate Partner of **hampstead**theatre's Russi:
The President's Holiday, 3 Sisters on Hope Street

❖ SALANS

hampsteadtheatre and Liverpool Everyman and Playhouse present

3 sisters on hope street

by **Diane Samuels** and **Tracy-Ann Oberman**, after **Anton Chekhov**

Cast

Tush	**Russell Bentley**
Arnold	**Ben Caplan**
Gertie Lasky	**Anna Francolini**
Mordy	**Elliot Levey**
Debbie	**Daisy Lewis**
Vince	**Finbar Lynch**
Solly	**Gerard Monaco**
Rita Lasky	**Samantha Robinson**
May Lasky	**Suzan Sylvester**
Auntie Beil	**Jennie Stoller**
Nate	**Philip Voss**

Creative Team

Director	**Lindsay Posner**
Designer	**Ruari Murchison**
Lighting Designer	**Peter Mumford**
Associate Lighting Designer	**Wayne Dowdeswell**
Sound Designer	**Matt McKenzie** for Autograph
Music Arranged & Performed by	**Jason Carr**
Costume Supervisor	**Jacquie Davies**
Voice/Dialect Coach	**Penny Dyer**
Casting Director	**Julia Horan**
Company Stage Manager	**Catryn Fray**
Deputy Stage Manager	**Leanne Fagan**
Assistant Stage Manager	**Maria Wells**
Set Built by	**Splinter**

For Liverpool Everyman and Playhouse
Production Manager **Sean Pritchard**
Sound Operator **Marc Williams**
Lighting Operator **Andy Webster**
Stage Crew **Howard Macaulay**
Dresser **James Theobald**

Press Officer **Pippa Taylor**
(0151 706 9100)

For **hampstead**theatre
Production Manager **Tom Albu**
Chief Electrician **Kim O'Donoghue**
Deputy Chief Electrician
Sherry Coenen
Technical Manager **David Tuff**
Deputy Technical Manager
Jonathan Goldstone
Press Officer **Becky Sayer**
(020 7449 4151)

hampsteadtheatre and Liverpool Everyman and Playhouse would like to thank:
Salisbury Playhouse
Truly Scrumptious Reborn Nursery for providing the doll (www.Truly-Scrumptious.biz)
Charlotte Heath
JNF UK for kindly supplying the blues boxes

3 Sisters on Hope Street was first performed on Friday 25 January 2008 at
the Everyman Theatre, Liverpool

cast and creative team

(*in alphabetical order*)

Russell Bentley (*Tush*)
Theatre includes: *Sit and Shiva* (Hackney Empire/New End Productions); *Chicken Soup with Barley* (Tricycle/Nottingham Playhouse); *Violent B* (Royal Court Young Writers Showcase); *Patience* (Activated Image/Finborough); *Spoils of War* (Young Vic Studio); *Tower of Bagel*, *Probe* (Soho Theatre); *Tutorials* (Jerwood Space/National Theatre Studio); *Waiting for Lefty* (winner of the James Menzies-Kitchen Directors Award), *The Cradle Will Rock* (BAC); *A Doll's House* (New End); *Angel* (Old Vic Young Voices Season); *Bitter Fruits of Palestine* (The John Caird Company); *Destiny of Me* (Finborough); *Old Wicked Songs* (Gielgud/Bristol Old Vic); *Roaring Lion* (Lyric Hammersmith). Television includes: *EastEnders*, *The Bill*, *Footballers' Wives Extra Time*, *Clitheroe*, *Cotton*, *The Eustace Brothers*, *Normandy*, *Late*, *First Among Equals*, *Cuban Conflict in America*, *Joy to the World*. Film includes: *Proof*, *Miramax*, *Below*, *Lost Battalion*, *Monday 10am*, *Biodiversity*. Radio includes: *Other Man*, *Ring Around the Bath*, *Goal*, *Voyage* (winner of Sony Talkies Award), *The Whore of Mensa*.

Ben Caplan (*Arnold*)
Theatre includes: *Two Thousand Years* (National Theatre); *Hamlet* (Nuffield, Southampton); *The Dwarfs* (Tricycle); *Romeo and Juliet*, *As You Like It*, *Sweat* (national tours); *Guys and Dolls*, *Les Grandes Meaulnes*, *Judging Billy Jones* (Young Vic). Television includes: *The Passion*, *Maxwell*, *The Candidate*, *Judge John Deed*, *Dwarfs*, *Band of Brothers*, *A Touch of Frost*, *Soldier, Soldier*, *Inspector Morse*, *The Perfect Blue*, *Where The Heart Is*. Film includes: *RocknRolla*.

Wayne Dowdeswell (Associate Lighting Designer)
Theatre designs include: *No More Sitting on the Old School Bench*, *A Man for All Seasons*, *Fanshen*, *Should Old Acquaintance* (Contact, Manchester); *Golden Girls*, *The Desert Air*, *Today*, *The Philistines*, *The Dillen* (RSC); *Deathwatch*, *The Maids*, *Speculators* (Pit Theatre, Barbican). As Lighting Supervisor at the RSC's Swan Theatre, designs include: *The Rover*, *The Fair Maid of the West*, *Hyde Park*, *Titus Andronicus*, *The Jew of Malta*, *Doctor Faustus*, *The Duchess of Malfi*, *Edward II*, *The Seagull*, *Tamburlaine the Great*, *The Country Wife*, *The Wives' Excuse*, *The Devil is an Ass*, *The Cherry Orchard*, *The Shakespeare Revue*, *The 'Jacobethan' Season*, *The Tamer Tamed*, *The 'Gunpowder' Season*, *Breakfast with Mugabe*, *The Canterbury Tales*. Other design work in the UK and overseas includes: *Not About Heroes*, *Macbeth*, *A Pin to See the Peep-Show*, *The Vanek Plays*, *Medea* (Wyndham's/ Broadway); *Sweeney Todd*, *The Caucasian Chalk Circle*, *The Trial*, *A Midsummer Night's Dream*, *The Mikado*, *Eugene Onegin*, *Rinaldo*, *The Birthday Party*, *Lucia di Lammermoor* (Scottish Opera); He received Olivier Award nominations for *Edward II* (Pit), *Tamburlaine the Great* (Barbican) and *Medea* (Wyndham's).

Anna Francolini (*Gertie Lasky*)
Theatre includes: *In the Club* (Hampstead); *Into the Woods* (Royal Opera House); *Caroline, Or Change* (National Theatre – Olivier Award nomination); *Six Pictures of Lee Miller* (Minerva, Chichester); *Anatol* (Arcola); *Spittin' Distance* (Stephen Joseph); *Romeo and Juliet* (English Touring Theatre); *The Ballad of Little Jo, Floyd Collins, Saturday Night* (Bridewell); *Things You Shouldn't Say Past Midnight* (Soho); *The Tempest* (A&BC Theatre Company); *Daisy Pulls It Off* (Lyric); *Mahler's Conversion* (Aldwych); *Merrily We Roll Along, Company* (Donmar); *A Midsummer Night's Dream* (Oxford Stage Company). Television includes: *Live Girls, Rome, Holby City, Lie with Me, Down to Earth, This Is Dom Joly, Jonathan Creek, Company, Mash & Peas Do US*. Film includes: *Topsy Turvy, The Final Curtain, The Barn, Z*.

Elliot Levey (*Mordy*)
Theatre includes: *Take Flight* (Menier Chocolate Factory); *How Much is Your Iron?, Monkey!, Tongue Tied* (Young Vic); *On Religion, On Ego* (Soho); *Henry IV Parts One & Two, His Dark Materials* (National Theatre); *Beasts and Beauties* (Bristol Old Vic); *The Tempest* (British Council tour/A & BC); *On Love* (Gate/RNT Studio); *Macbeth* (West End); *Comedy of Errors* (RSC); *The Reckless are Dying Out* (Lyric Hammersmith); *Tonight We Fly* (Trestle); *Arabian Nights, Milk and Blood, Lifted Up from Earth* (BAC); *The Soldier's Tale* (Theatre Artaud); *The Warp* (Three Mills Island); *Cyrano de Bergerac* (Bridewell); *Perdition* (Gate); Film and television includes: *Last Chance Harvey, Filth and Wisdom, Sex and the City, The Queen, Song of Songs, Beau Brummell, Casualty 1906, EastEnders, Holby City, Supertex, Judas and Jesus, The Book of John, Jason and the Argonauts, Jesus, Amnesia, Lump in My Throat, Sirens, Fat Friends, Lovejoy*. Radio includes: *Love's Work* (Radio 4); *Radetsky March* (Radio 3).

Daisy Lewis (*Debbie*)
Theatre includes: *The Good Family* (Royal Court); *Silence* (NYT/Wiltons); *Blue Moon Over Poplar* (NYT/Soho); *Antigone at Hell's Mouth* (NYT/Kneehigh). Television includes: *Miss Austen Regrets, After You've Gone, Doctor Who*.

Finbar Lynch (*Vince*)
Theatre includes: *The Hothouse, Antony and Cleopatra, King Lear* (National Theatre); *Ghosts* (Gate); *The Tempest, Julius Caesar, Measure for Measure, Coriolanus, The Alchemist, The Virtuoso, Amphibians, A Women Killed With Kindness, The Two Gentleman of Verona, Julius Caesar* (RSC); *As You Desire Me* (Playhouse, London); *The Birthday Party* (Duchess, London); *Hecuba, To the Green Fields Beyond, Fool for Love, Translations* (Donmar); *Othello, Miss Julie* (Greenwich); *Macbeth* (Sheffield Crucible); *Messiah* (Riverside Studios/tour); *A Moon for the Misbegotten* (Manchester Royal Exchange); *Not About Nightingales* (National/Broadway – Tony Nomination for Best Supporting Actor, Drama Desk nomination Best Actor, 1999); *Three Sisters* (Royal Court/Gate, Dublin); *A Midsummer Night's Dream* (RSC/Broadway); *Playboy of the Western World, All the Way Back, The Silver Dollar Boys*

(Abbey); *Philadelphia Here I Come, Noises Off, Mass Appeal, Death of a Salesman* (Gaiety); *Juno and the Paycock* (Milwaukee Rep); *The Rivals, School For Scandal, Fathers and Sons, Absurd Person Singular, A Streetcar Named Desire, Peer Gynt* (Gate Dublin – Best Actor, Irish Theatre Awards). Television includes: *Proof* (Series 1 and 2), *Dalziel and Pascoe, Glenroe* (series 1– 4), *Waking the Dead, Red Cap, Attila the Hun, Second Sight, Mind Games, Holby City, Small World, Between the Lines. George Gently, The Eejits.* Film includes: *Matilde, To Kill a King, Lost Battalion, King Lear, Scold's Bridle, A Midsummer Night's Dream, The Schooner, The Wild Ponies, A Secret Audience.*

Matt McKenzie (Sound Designer)
As sound designer, theatre includes: *The Giant* (Hampstead); *Favourite Nights, Rents, Brittanicus, Noises Off, The White Glove, The Provok'd Wife, Private Dick, Miss Julie, Hobson's Choice, Mass Appeal, Crime and Punishment, Lent and the Man Who Fell in Love with his Wife, Angry Housewives, The Hypochondriac, Faith Hope and Charity, Sailor Beware, Loot, Lady Audley's Secret, Madras House, The Way of the World, Ghost Train, Greasepaint, In the Summer House, Exact Change* (Lyric Hammersmith); *Macbeth* (Nuffield, Southampton); *Una Pooka* (Tricycle); *Vertigo, That Good Night, Hinge of the World* (Guildford); *Saturday Sunday Monday, Easy Virtue, The Seagull, A Midsummer Night's Dream, The Master and Margarita, 5/11, Nicholas Nickleby* (Chichester Festival); *Dracula, Frankenstein, A Midsummer Night's Dream, Macbeth* (Derby Playhouse); *Flamingos, Damages, After the End* (Bush); *Made in Bangkok, The House of Bernarda Alba, A Piece of My Mind, Journey's End, A Madhouse in Goa, Barnaby and the Old Boys, Irma Vep, Gasping, Map of the Heart, Tango Argentino, When She Danced, Misery, Murder Is Easy, The Odd Couple, Pygmalion, Things We Do For Love, Long Day's Journey into Night, Macbeth, Sexual Perversity in Chicago, Calico, A Life in the Theatre, Swimming with Sharks* (West End); *Lysistrata, The Master Builder, School for Wives, Mind Millie for Me, A Streetcar Named Desire, Three of a Kind* (Sir Peter Hall); *Amadeus* (Sir Peter Hall/West End/Broadway); *Leaves of Glass, Baghdad Wedding* (Soho); *Frame 312, After Miss Julie, Days of Wine and Roses* (Donmar); *Iron, The People Next Door* (The Traverse). He was Sound Supervisor for the Peter Hall Seasons at the Old Vic and the Piccadilly, and designed the sound for *Waste, Cloud Nine, The Seagull, The Provok'd Wife, King Lear, The Misanthrope, Major Barbara, Filumena, Kafka's Dick, Family Reunion, Henry V, The Duchess of Malfi, Hamlet, The Lieutenant of Inishmore, Julius Caesar, A Midsummer Night's Dream* (RSC). Matt's musical work includes: *Love Off the Shelf* (Nuffield, Southampton); *The Bells are Ringing, Talk of the Steamie* (Greenwich); *Forbidden Broadway, Blues in the Night* (West End); Matthew Bourne's *Car Man* (West End/international tour); *Putting it Together, The Gondoliers, How to Succeed in Business Without Really Trying, Carousel, Babes in Arms* (Chichester); *Oh! What A Lovely War, A Christmas Carol, Sweeney Todd, Company, Into the Woods, Merrily We Roll Along, Moon Landing* (Derby Playhouse); Mark Ravenhill's *Dick Whittington* (Barbican).

Gerard Monaco (*Solly*)
Theatre includes: *The Rose Tattoo* (National Theatre); *The Lady Killers* (Northcott); *Albert's Boy* (Finborough); *Biloxi Blues* (Vanbrugh); *How I Got That Story* (Finborough); *Pool Death* (Salisbury Playhouse). Television includes: *The Passion, Little Miss Jocelyn, Honest, Holby City, Hindenburg, Rome, EastEnders, The Bill, The Inspector Lynley Mysteries, As If*. Film includes: *Starter for Ten, Vera Drake*.

Peter Mumford (Lighting Designer)
Theatre includes: *Shadowlands* (Wyndham's); *Fiddler on the Roof* (Savoy); *The Hothouse, The Rose Tattoo, The Reporter, Exiles, The Talking Cure, Bacchai, Vincent in Brixton, Luther, Summerfolk* (National Theatre); *Amy's View* (Garrick); *A Voyage Round My Father* (Donmar/West End); *Cloud Nine, Hedda Gabler, The Goat or Who is Sylvia?* (Almeida); *The Seagull, Drunk Enough to Say I Love You?, Dying City* (Royal Court); *The Last Confession* (Chichester Festival/West End); *The Entertainer, Richard II* (Old Vic); *Summer and Smoke, Waiting for Godot, You Never Can Tell* (West End); *Private Lives, Pygmalion* (Theatre Royal Bath); *Brand, Macbeth, Hamlet* (RSC); *Private Lives* (West End/Broadway); *Sleeping Beauty, Cinderella, The Nutcracker, 32 Cryptograms* (Scottish Ballet). Opera includes: *Madama Butterfly* (English National Opera/The Metropolitan Opera House, NYC); *Eugene Onegin* (Royal Opera House/Finnish Opera); *La Cenerentola* (Glyndebourne); *The Midsummer Marriage* (Lyric Opera Chicago); *Passion* (Minnesota Opera); *Così Fan Tutte, Die Soldaten, The Coronation of Poppea* (ENO); *Il Trovatore* (Paris); *La Traviata* (Antwerp); *La Boheme; The Magic Flute* (Vilnius); *Siegfried, Götterdämmerung , Fidelio, Don Giovanni* (Scottish Opera); *Katya Kabanova, Madama Butterfly* (Opera North); *Giulio Cesare* (Bordeaux); *Eugine Onegin, The Bartered Bride* (ROH). He directed and designed John Luther Adams' *Earth and the Great Weather* (Almeida Opera) and co-directed and designed the sets and lighting for *L'Heure Espagnole* and *L'Enfant et les Sortilèges* (Opera Zuid). Television includes directing: *48 Preludes and Fugues* (Bach) series for BBC2, many dance/music films for BBC and C4 and most recently was director of photography for *The Little Prince* (BBC2). He won the Olivier Award for Outstanding Achievement in Dance (1995) and the Olivier for Best Lighting (*Bacchai*, National Theatre) in 2003.

Ruari Murchison (Designer)
Theatre designs include: *The Glass Room, Gone to L.A.* (Hampstead); *The Grouch, Macbeth, Alice in Wonderland, The Lion, the Witch and the Wardrobe, Electricity, Medea* (West Yorkshire Playhouse); *Intemperance* (Liverpool Everyman); *Alfie* (Watford Palace); *Dracula* (Churchill Theatre, Bromley); *Solid Gold Cadillac* (Garrick/Yvonne Arnaud); *Mappa Mundi, Frozen, The Waiting Room, The Red Balloon* (National Theatre); *Titus Andronicus* (RSC); *A Busy Day* (Lyric, Shaftesbury Avenue); *Peggy Sue Got Married* (Shaftesbury); *The Snowman* (Peacock); *Henry IV Parts 1 & 2* (Washington Shakespeare Company, USA); *West Side Story, The Sound of Music* (Stratford Festival, Canada); *Hamlet* (Elisnore, Denmark); *Mrs Warren's Profession, The Threepenny Opera, An Enemy of the People*

(Theatr Clwyd); *Uncle Vanya*, *The Soldier's Tale*, *A Doll's House*, the David Hare Trilogy: *Racing Demon*, *Absence of War*, *Murmuring Judges* (TMA Best Design Nomination 2003), *The Tempest*, *Macbeth*, *The Merchant of Venice*, *Hamlet*, *Frozen*, *The Four Alice Bakers*, *Jumpers*, *Nativity*, *Translations*, *Big Maggie*, *Playing by the Rules*, *A Wedding Story* (Birmingham Rep); *Sweet Little Thing*, *Dracula*, *Twelfth Night*, *Hamlet*, *The Merchant of Venice*, *Romeo and Juliet*, *A Wedding Story*, *A Doll's House* (national tours). Opera designs include: *Peter Grimes*, *Così Fan Tutte* (Luzerner Opera, Switzerland); *La Cenerentola*, *Il Barbiere di Siviglia* (Garsington); *L'Italiana in Algeri* (Buxton); *Les Pèlerins à la Mecque*, *ZaZa* (Wexford); *The Magic Flute*, *A Midsummer Night's Dream* (Covent Garden Festival). Ballet designs include: *Landschaft und Erinnerung* (Stuttgart Ballett, Germany); *The Protecting Veil* (Birmingham Royal Ballet); *Le Festin de l'Araignée* (Royal Ballet School/ Royal Opera House Gala) – all choreographed by David Bintley.

Tracy-Ann Oberman (Writer)

Tracy-Ann is a television and theatre actor and writer. After studying Drama and Literature at Manchester University, Tracy-Ann trained at Central School of Speech and Drama, including a term at The Moscow Arts Theatre School, where the idea for *3 Sisters on Hope Street* was formed. As an actor Tracy-Ann has had a wide and varied career. Her theatre credits include working with the Royal Shakespeare Company, the National Theatre, Chichester Festival Theatre and Minerva, Soho Theatre, West Yorkshire Playhouse, Southwark Playhouse, and the Vaudeville and Comedy Theatres in the West End. Theatre includes: *Boeing Boeing* (Comedy); *The Oak Tree*, *School Play* (Soho); *Edmond* (National Theatre); *Loot* (Chichester Festival/Vaudeville); *Saturday Sunday Monday* (Chichester Festival); *Hello and Goodbye* (Southwark). For Television credits include: Chrissie Watts in *EastEnders*, Amy in *Sorted*, Yvonne Hartman in *Doctor Who* (series 2), *Big Train* (series 2) (all BBC); Beverley in *Bob Martin* (ITV, series 1 and 2), *Marion and Geoff* (A Small Party); *Happiness*, *Rhona*, *The Way It Is*, *Lenny Henry in Pieces*, *Paul Kaye Show*, *Strangerers*, *The Bill*, *Kiss Me Kate*, *Casualty*, *The Grove*, *Bromwell High*. Film includes: *An Hour in Paradise*, *Killing Time*, *The Cow*. She has been in over 600 radio drama, comedy and sketch shows on BBC Radio 4. As a presenter she has reviewed for *Jonathan Ross Film 2006*. She has performed as a stand-up comedian. *3 Sisters on Hope Street* is her first writing project for the stage. She has also written numerous comedy sketches for television, a BBC award-winning sitcom for BBC3, *The Harringham Harker*, written and starred in a number of episodes of *Big Train* (BBC2), and has been a regular columnist for the *Guardian*. She has had a number of short stories published.

Lindsay Posner (Director)

Lindsay has most recently directed *Fiddler on the Roof* which is currently playing at the Savoy Theatre in the West End, having transferred from the Sheffield Crucible. Theatre includes: *Fool for Love* (Apollo); *Tom and Viv*, *The Hypochondriac*, *Romance* (Almeida); *The Birthday Party* (Duchess); *A Life in the Theatre* (Apollo); *Oleanna*

(Garrick); *Dada: Man and Boy*, composed by Michael Nyman (Almeida/New Jersey); the world premiere of *Power*, *Tartuffe* (National Theatre); *The Caretaker* (Bristol Old Vic); *Sexual Perversity in Chicago* (Comedy); *Twelfth Night*, *The Rivals*, *Volpone*, *The Taming of the Shrew* (RSC); *The Misanthrope*, *American Buffalo* (Young Vic); *After Darwin* (Hampstead); *The Provok'd Wife* (Old Vic); *The Lady from the Sea* (Lyric Hammersmith/West Yorkshire Playhouse); *The Seagull* (Gate, Dublin); *The Robbers* (Gate). Lindsay was associate director at the Royal Court Theatre from 1987 to 1992 where his production of *Death and the Maiden* won two Laurence Olivier Awards. Other productions at the Royal Court include: *Colquhoun and McBryde*, *The Treatment*, *American Bagpipes* (Theatre Downstairs); *Ficky Stingers*, *No One Sees the Video*, *Built on Sand*, *Blood*, *Downfall*, *Ambulance* (Theatre Upstairs). Opera includes: *Love Counts* (Almeida); *Guilio Cesaré* (Royal Opera House at the Barbican); *Jenufa* (Opera Theatre Company, Dublin); *Dada: Man and Boy* (Almeida/Montclair Theatre, USA).

Samantha Robinson (*Rita Lasky*)
Theatre includes: *The Tempest* (Royal Exchange, Manchester); *The Three Musketeers* (Bristol Old Vic/New Vic); *A Taste of Honey* (Oldham Coliseum/tour); *The Laramie Project* (Sound, Leicester Square); *The Lemon Princess* (West Yorkshire Playhouse); *The Owl Service* (Plymouth Theatre Royal); *Untouchable* (Bush); *Song of the Western Men* (Chichester Festival). Television includes: *Holby City*, *Shameless*, *The Girls Who Came to Stay*, *Island at War*, *Final Demand*. Film includes: *Sixty Six*, *Jamaica Me Crazy*. Radio includes: *Life with Lisa*, *Evaristo's Epitaph*.

Diane Samuels (Writer)
Diane Samuels was born in Liverpool. The Jewish community of her upbringing informed her work on *3 Sisters on Hope Street*. She now lives in London where she has been writing extensively as a dramatist and author for nearly twenty years. *Kindertransport* won the Verity Bargate and Meyer-Whitworth awards and was first produced by Soho Theatre Company in 1993. It has since been performed in the West End, Off Broadway and all over the world, revived in 2007 in a highly acclaimed production by Shared Experience Theatre Company. For younger audiences, her play *How to Beat a Giant* completed a successful run in autumn 2007 at the Unicorn Theatre, for whom she is also writing *Echo and Dorian*, a contemporary take on Wilde's *The Picture of Dorian Gray*. Diane has wide experience of teaching creative writing, lecturing at the universities of Birmingham, Reading, Oxford, and at Goldsmiths College, London. She runs a regular writers' group and is writer-in-residence at Grafton Primary School in Islington, north London. Diane was one of a creative team awarded a Science on Stage and Screen Award by the Welcome Trust in 2001. The resulting work, *PUSH*, was performed at The People Show Studios in London in June 2003. Her short story, *Rope* was one of the winners in BBC Radio 4's online short story competition, broadcast in 2002. As Pearson Creative Research Fellow 2004/5 at the British Library, she completed research into magic, and her booklet *A Writer's Magic Notebook* was published in 2006. She is currently

working on *Swine* at the National Theatre Studio and developing a new project with Shared Experience. Diane writes for the *Jewish Quarterly* and regularly reviews books for the *Guardian*.

Jennie Stoller (*Auntie Beil*)
Theatre includes: *Playing Sinatra* (New End); *Woyzeck* (Gate); *The Oedipus Plays, Mountain Giants, Harliquinade, The Elephant Man* (National Theatre); *Ion* (National Theatre Studio); *A Midsummer Night's Dream, The Beaux Stratagem* (RSC/tour); *The Europeans, The Castle* (The Wrestling School/Riverside/Berlin/Paris/tour – Best Actress In a Visiting Production Award Manchester Evening News); *Brighton Beach Memoirs* (West Yorkshire Playhouse); *The House of Bernarda Alba* (Royal Lyceum, Edinburgh); *Heartbreak House* (Shared Experience); *The Henry's* (ESC Old Vic/Toronto/tour); *Cries from the Mammal House, Fen* (Royal Court/Public Theatre NYC); *The Merchant of Venice, As You Like It* (ACTOR tours USA); Helena in Peter Brook's *A Midsummer Night's Dream* (RSC/World tour). Television includes: *Casualty, In Defence, McLibel, Bliss, The Way We Used to Live, Scott of the Arms Antics* (Royal Society Television Award), *One Foot In The Grave, Love Hurts, The Bill, Shrinks, Two's Company, Sapphire and Steel*, and the title role in *Eleanor Marx*. Film includes: *King Ralph, The Good Father*. Radio includes: Member of BBC RDC 2001. Has performed in over 80 broadcasts, including *Seven Wonders of the Divided World, Shylock, Maigret, Little Dorrit, Love, The Amber Spyglass, Orlando*. Writing contributions include: *Stagecraft* (chapter on acting), *The Joint Stock Book, Theatre in Nicaragua* (article for the *Guardian*).

Suzan Sylvester (*May Lasky*)
Theatre includes: *Othello* (Salisbury Playhouse); *Heartbreak House* (Watford); *Black Milk, Terrorism, Cleansed* (Royal Court); *Crooked, Little Baby Nothing, Shangalang, Card Boys* (Bush); *The Santaland Diaries* (Birmingham Rep); *Frankie and Johnny in the Clair de Lune* (Sound Theatre); *Tabloid Caligula* (Arcola, London/59th Street, New York); *The Real Thing* (tour); *The Secret Rapture, Three Sisters* (Chichester); *Betrayal* (Northcott, Exeter); *Terms of Abuse* (Hampstead); *House of Bernarda Alba* (Theatr Clywd); *The Reckless are Dying Out* (Lyric Hammersmith); *All My Sons, The Glass Menagerie, Romeo and Juliet* (Young Vic); *Enemy of the People* (Young Vic/Playhouse); *As You Like It, The Government Inspector, The Seagull* (Crucible); *Kindertransport, Yiddish Trojan Women* (Soho); *Life Is A Dream* (West Yorkshire Playhouse); *Love's Labours Lost* (Royal Exchange, Manchester); *Pericles, All's Well That Ends Well* (RSC); *'Tis Pity She's a Whore, A Small Family Business* (National Theatre); *A View from the Bridge* (National Theatre/transferred to the Aldwych – Best Newcomer Olivier Award). Television includes: *Kingdom, EastEnders, Holby City, Silent Witness, The Quatermass Experiment, Family Affairs, Doctors, The Bill, Casualty, Where the Heart Is, Maisie Raine, A Touch of Frost, London's Burning, Holding On, Wycliffe, Pie in the Sky, Peak Practice, Rides, Call Me Mister, Misterioso*. Film includes: *Streets of Yesterday, Bilingual*. Radio Includes: *Macbeth, Pentecost, The Rover, The Last Day*.

Philip Voss (*Nate*)

Philip Voss is an Associate Actor of the RSC and among the roles he has played for that company are Prospero, Malvolio, Shylock, Menenius in *Coriolanus*, Cardinal Monticelso in *The White Devil*, Sir Epicure Mammon in *The Alchemist*, Peter Quince in *A Midsummer Night's Dream* and Ulysses in *Troilus and Cressida*. For the Royal National Theatre: Rodin in *The Wandering Jew*, Ferdinando in *Countrymania*, James in *The Strangeness of Others*, Juster in *Abingdon Square*, Count Shabelsky in *Ivanov*, Boyet in Sir Trevor Nunn's productions of *Love's Labour's Lost*, Miguel Estete in *The Royal Hunt of the Sun*. His other work in London includes: for Shared Experience – Doctor Dorn in *The Seagull*, Dr Chebutykin in *Three Sisters*, and Kochkaryov in *Marriage*. For Sir Peter Hall: *The Royal Family*, *Much Ado About Nothing* and Jaques in *As You Like It*, both in England and America. He performed at the original Hampstead Theatre in *Short List* by Michael Rudman and *Particular Friendships* by Martyn Allen (directed respectively by Mike Ockrent and Michael Attenborough), and most recently at the new Hampstead Theatre in *The Giant* by Sir Antony Sher. Film includes: *Brides in the Bath*, *The Dwelling Place*, *Let Them Eat Cake*, *Octopussy*, *Four Weddings and a Funeral*, *Frankenstein and the Monster from Hell*. Recent radio includes: Simon Gray's *Little Nell*.

hampsteadtheatre

hampsteadtheatre is one of the UK's leading new-writing venues housed in a magnificent purpose-built state-of-the-art theatre – a company that is fast approaching its fiftieth year of operation.

hampsteadtheatre has a mission: to find, develop, and produce new plays to the highest possible standards, for as many people as we can encourage to see them. Its work is both national and international in its scope and ambition.

hampsteadtheatre exists to take risks and to discover the talent of the future. New writing is our passion. We consistently create the best conditions for writers to flourish and are rewarded with diverse award-winning and far-reaching plays.

The list of playwrights who had their early work produced at **hampstead**theatre who are now filling theatres all over the country and beyond include Mike Leigh, Michael Frayn, Brian Friel, Terry Johnson, Hanif Kureishi, Simon Block, Abi Morgan, Rona Munro, Tamsin Oglesby, Harold Pinter, Philip Ridley, Shelagh Stephenson, debbie tucker green, Crispin Whittell, Tamsin Oglesby and Roy Williams. Most recently it has produced award-winning plays by Nell Leyshon, Dennis Kelly and James Philips.

Each year the theatre invites the most exciting writers around to write for us. At least half of these playwrights will be emerging writers who are just hitting their stride – writers who we believe are on the brink of establishing themselves as important new voices. We also ask mid-career and mature playwrights to write for us on topics they are burning to explore.

hampsteadtheatre gratefully acknowledges the support of

ARTS COUNCIL ENGLAND

LONDON COUNCILS

Camden
Funded by Camden Council

hampsteadtheatre's role as one of the finest new writing venues in London is made possible by the generous support of our Luminary members. We would like to thank the following individuals and companies for ensuring the future of our artistic and educational programmes.

our current luminaries are:

(as of January 2008)

thank you to the following for supporting our creativity:

Abbey Charitable Trust; Acacia Charitable Trust; The Andor Charitable Trust; Anglo American; Arimathea Charitable Trust; Arts & Business; Awards for All; Auerbach Trust Charity; Bank Leumi; BBC Children in Need; The Basil Samuels Charitable Trust; Bennetts Associates; Big Lottery Fund; Blick Rothenberg; Bridge House Estates Trust Fund; The Chapman Charitable Trust; Swiss Cottage Area Partnership; Community Fund; The John S Cohen Foundation; Coutts Charitable Trust; D'Oyly Carte Charitable Trust; The Dorset Foundation; Duis Charitable Trust; The Eranda Foundation; The Ernest Cook Trust; European Association of Jewish Culture; Garrick Charitable Trust; Gerald Ronson Foundation; The Hampstead & Highgate Express; Hampstead, Wells & Campden Trust; Help a London Child; Harold Hyam Wingate Foundation; The Jack Petchey Foundation; Jacobs Charitable Trust; John Lyon's Charity Trust; Kennedy Leigh Charitable Trust; Local Network Fund; Mackintosh Foundation; Markson Pianos; Marriot Hotel, Regents Park; Milly Apthorp Charitable Trust; The Morel Trust: The Noël Coward Foundation; Notes Productions Ltd; Parkheath Estates: The Paul Hamlyn Foundation; Pembertons Property Management; The Rayne Foundation; Reed Elsevier; Richard Reeves Foundation; Royal Victoria Hall Foundation; Salans; Samuel French; The Shoresh Foundation; Society for Theatre Research; Solomon Taylor Shaw: Sweet and Maxwell; Karl Sydow; Towry Law; The Vandervell Foundation; The Vintners' Company; World Jewish Relief; Charles Wolfson Foundation; Zurich Community Trust.

If you would like to become more closely involved, and would like to help us find the talent and the audiences of the future, please call Tamzin Robertson on 020 7449 4171 or email development@hampsteadtheatre.com

capital campaign supporters

hampsteadtheatre would like to thank the following donors who kindly contributed to the Capital Campaign, enabling us to build our fantastic new home.

Mr Robert Adams
Mr Robert Ainscow
Mrs Farah Alaghband
Mr W Aldwinckle
Mr Mark Allison
Anonymous
Mrs Klari Atkin
Mr William Atkins
Mr and Mrs Daniel and Pauline Auerbach
Mr David Aukin
Sir Alan Ayckbourn
Mr George Bailey
Mr Christopher Beard
Mr Eric Beecham
Mrs Lucy Ben-Levi
Mr Alan Bennett
Mr and Mrs Rab Bennetts
Mr Roger Berlind
Ms Vicky Biles
Mr Michael Blakemore
Mr Simon Block
Mr A Bloomfield
Mr John Bolton
Mr Peter Borender
Mr and Mrs Rob and Colleen Brand
Mr Matthew Broadbent
Mr Alan Brodie
Dr John and Dorothy Brook
Mr Leonard Bull
Mr and Mrs Paul and Ossie Burger
Ms Kathy Burke
Mr O Burstin
Ms Deborah Buzan
Mr Charles Caplin
Sir Trevor and Susan Chinn
Mr Martin Cliff
Mr Michael Codron
Mr and Mrs Denis Cohen
Dr David Cohen
Mr David Cornwell
Mr and Mrs Sidney and Elizabeth Corob
Mr and Mrs John Crosfield
Miss Nicci Crowther
Ms Hilary Dane
Mr and Mrs Ralph Davidson
Mr and Mrs Gerald Davidson
Mrs Deborah Davis
Mr Edwin Davison
Mr David Day
Ms Frankie de Freitas
Mr and Mrs David and Jose Dent
Professor Christopher and Elizabeth Dickinson

Sir Harry Djanogly
Ms Lindsay Duncan
Mr David Dutton
Mrs Myrtle Ellenbogen
Mr Michael Elwyn
Mr Tom Erhardt
Sir Richard Eyre
Mr Peter Falk
Ms Nina Finburgh
Mr and Mrs George and Rosamund Fokschaner
Ms Lisa Forrell
Mr N Forsyth
Mr Freddie Fox
Mr Michael Frayn
Mr Norman Freed
Mr Conrad Freedman
Mr and Mrs Robert and Elizabeth Freeman
Mr and Mrs Jeremy and Susan Freeman
Mr and Mrs Brian Friel
Mr Arnold Fulton
Mr and Mrs Michael and Jacqueline Gee
Mr and Mrs Jonathan and Jacqueline Gestetner
Mr Desmond Goch
Mr Anthony Goldstein
Mr Andrew Goodman
Ms Niki Gorick
Mrs Katerina Gould
Lord and Lady Grabiner
Mr and Mrs Jonathan Green
Mr and Mrs David Green
Mrs Susan Green
Mr Nicholas Greenstone
Mr Michael Gross
Mr and Mrs Paul Hackworth
Dr Peter and Elaine Hallgarten
Miss Susan Hampshire
Mr Christopher Hampton
Mr Laurence Harbottle
Sir David Hare
Lady Pamela Harlech
Mr Paul Harris
Mr John Harrison
Mr Howard Harrison
Mr Jonathan Harvey
Sir Maurice Hatter
Mr Marc Hauer
Dr Samuel Hauer
Mr and Mrs Michael and Morven Heller
Mr Philip Hobbs
Mr and Mrs Robin and Inge Hyman
Mr Nicholas Hytner

Ms Phoebe Isaacs
Mr Michael Israel
Professor Howard and Sandra Jacobs
Mr and Mrs Max Jacobs
Dr C Kaplanis
Mrs Patricia Karet
Baroness Helena Kennedy
Mrs Ann Kieran
Mr Jeremy King
Mr Peter Knight
Sir Eddie Kulukundis
Ms Belinda Lang
Mr and Mrs Edward Lee
Mrs Janette Lesser
Lady Diane Lever
Mr Daniel Levy
Mr Peter Levy
Sir Sydney and Lady Lipworth
Mrs Alyssa Lovegrove
Ms Sue MacGregor
Mr S Magee
Mr Fouad Malouf
Mr and Mrs Lee Manning
Mr and Mrs Thomas and Karen Mautner
Mr and Mrs David and Sandra Max
Mrs June McCall
Mr John McFadden
Mr Ewan McGregor
Mr and Mrs David Meller
Mr Raymond Mellor
Mr Anthony Minghella
Mr and Mrs David Mirvish
Mr and Mrs Mark Mishon
Mr and Mrs Edward and Diana Mocatta
Mr and Mrs Gary Monnickendam
Mrs and Mrs David and Sandra Montague
Mr Peter Morris
Mr and Mrs Ian Morrison
Mr Andrew Morton
Lady Sara Morton
Mr Gabriel Moss QC
Mr and Mrs Terence Mugliston
Mr and Mrs Roger and Bridget Myddelton
Mr Stewart Nash
Mr James Nederlander
Mr John Newbigin
Sir Trevor Nunn
Mr T Owen
Mr and Mrs Simon and Midge Palley
Mr Barrie Pearson

for **hampstead**theatre

About the Liverpool and Everyman Playhouse

Liverpool has an illustrious theatrical heritage, with the Everyman and Playhouse producing many of this country's most acclaimed writers, performers and theatre-makers. Since January 2004, we have been continually in production, creating shows which have ensured that 'Made in Liverpool' is widely recognised as a stamp of theatrical quality.

This homegrown programme has won national acclaim and extraordinarily loyal audiences by offering fresh and exciting productions of great plays at the Playhouse, while, at the Everyman, nurturing and producing a prodigious range of new Liverpool plays. Many Everyman and Playhouse productions have toured nationally and transferred to London and Edinburgh, and Liverpool's presence on the national theatrical map is a vibrant and inspiring one.

Around our in-house productions, we host some of the finest touring companies from around the country, to offer a rich and varied programme for the people of Liverpool and Merseyside, and for the increasing number of visitors to our city.

But there is more to these theatres than simply the work on our stages. We have a busy literary department, working to nurture the next generation of Liverpool Playwrights. A wide-ranging community department takes our work to all corners of the city and surrounding areas, and works in partnership with schools, colleges, youth and community groups to open up the theatre to all. The Everyman and Playhouse Youth Theatre trains and develops the theatrical talent of the future. The Youth Theatre recently staged their first full length production; *Julius Caesar* at the Everyman.

Our aim is for these theatres to be an engine for creative excellence, artistic adventure, and audience involvement; firmly rooted in our community, yet both national and international in scope and ambition.

'*...a theatrical renaissance on Merseyside*' The Observer

2008 European Capital of Culture

Liverpool is a city with a big heart; indomitable, irrepressible, and a city known the world over for its great Liverpool icons and strong personality. The Everyman and Playhouse theatres' 'Made in Liverpool' programme in 2008 includes several new commissions, all infused with this unique spirit of the city while being created for the national and international stage.

We are delighted that our first production of 2008 is this co-production with Hampstead Theatre of a vibrant new take on Chekhov's *Three Sisters*. *3 Sisters on Hope Street* is the opening fanfare to our 2008 programme and raises the curtain on Part I of our year-long carnival of culture.

Also in Part I we welcome back Everyman Alumnus Matthew Kelly who will appear alongside his son Matthew Rixon in Lucy Pitman-Wallace's production of Samuel Beckett's *Endgame*.

In Part II our programme takes on a musical note. *Once Upon a Time at the Adelphi* is a new musical comedy, taking an irreverent but affectionate look at one of Liverpool's iconic buildings and its extraordinary history. Writer and director Phil Willmott has spent the last twelve months gathering stories before choosing the setting of movie stars and 1930s Liverpool; the musical theme continues into Part III when *Eric's - The Musical* sees another Liverpool icon coming under the spotlight from Liverpool writer Mark Davies Markham. *Eric's* will celebrate this musical hothouse of the late seventies-early eighties when The Clash, The Ramones and The Sex Pistols ignited a creative spark that fired a generation.

Another Everyman alumnus returns when Pete Postlethwaite is *King Lear*, joining creative forces again with award-winning director Rupert Goold in a co-production with Headlong Theatre in a fitting return to the theatre that launched Postlethwaite's exceptional career.

The theatres have been liaising with the very best touring companies for 2008, including Out of Joint, Lyric Hammersmith, the Donmar Warehouse, Shared Experience, Northern Broadsides and the RSC.

The Playhouse is host to some of the best international dance companies in March as part of the annual LEAP festival of dance with the European première of world renowned British choreographer Akram Khan's *bahok*, and New York's hottest dance company, the all-female Decadancetheatre with their hip-hop ballet *Firebird*.

Full details of our 2008 programme as well as further exciting announcements throughout the year can be found on our website at **www.everymanplayhouse.com** or for more information on Part I pick up one of our handy, pocket-sized guides from our Box Office.

CELEBRATE LIVERPOOL. CELEBRATE CULTURE. CELEBRATE 08.

The theatre's 2008 programme is supported by The Liverpool Culture Company as part of the 2008 European Capital of Culture

New Writing at the Liverpool Everyman and Playhouse

'The Everyman is back producing the next generation of Liverpool playwrights.' (The Guardian)

At the beating heart of the theatre's renaissance is our work with writers; since it is our passionate belief that an investment in new writing is an investment in our theatrical future.

'The Everyman's new writing programme has unearthed a talent worth celebrating.' (The Guardian on *Intemperance* by Lizzie Nunnery)

In just over two years, the theatres will have produced ten world premières of plays developed and nurtured in Liverpool – most recently including *Intemperance* by Lizzie Nunnery, *The May Queen* by Stephen Sharkey, *The Electric Hills* by Michael McLean, *The Flint Street Nativity* by Tim Firth, *The Way Home* by Chlöe Moss and *Unprotected* by Esther Wilson, John Fay, Tony Green and Lizzie Nunnery, which transferred to the Edinburgh Festival where it won the Amnesty International Freedom of Expression Award.

'The Everyman in Liverpool is living up to its name. Thanks to a new play, it is doing what theatres all over the country dream of: pulling in scores of first-time theatregoers alongside loyal subscribers… blazes with energetic intelligence… this will change people's minds and in unexpected ways.' (The Observer on *Unprotected*)

As we celebrate European Capital of Culture 2008, the theatres have a variety of exciting projects which grow on the foundations of recent work.

Around the main production programme, the theatres run a range of projects and activities to create opportunities and endeavour to support writers at every career stage. The commissioning programme invests in the creation of new work for both the Everyman and Playhouse stages.

The Young Writer's Programme is a year-long programme working alongside experienced practitioners, which nurtures and develops exciting new voices to create a new generation of Liverpool writers. An annual new writing festival, Everyword, offers a busy and popular week of seminars, sofa talks and work-in-progress readings.

For more information about the Everyman and Playhouse – including the full programme, off-stage activities such as Playwright Support, and ways in which you can support our investment in talent – visit www.everymanplayhouse.com

With Thanks

Liverpool Everyman and Playhouse would like to thank all our current funders:

Corporate Members A C Robinson and Associates, Barbara McVey, Beetham, Benson Signs, Brabners Chaffe Street, Chadwick Chartered Accountants, Downtown Liverpool in Business, Duncan Sheard Glass, DWF, EEF North West, Grant Thornton, Hope Street Hotel, Mando Group, Morgenrot Chevalier, Synergy, The Mersey Partnership, Victor Huglin Carpets, Lime Pictures, Concept Communications, Crushed Apple, Lloyds TSB, Uniform, 7 Harrington Chambers, Bruntwood, Morecroft Solicitors.

Trusts and Foundations The PH Holt Charitable Trust, The Liverpool Culture Company, The Rex Makin Charitable Trust, Malcolm and Roger Frood in memory of Graham and Joan Frood, Riverside Charitable Trust, Liverpool Housing Trust, Liverpool East Neighbourhood Management Services, CDS/Plus One, South Central Neighbourhood Management Services, Arena Housing, Isle of Man Arts Council, Unity Trust, Mary Webb Trust, Robert Kiln Trust, Margaret Guido Trust, N. Smith Charitable Trust.

This theatre has the support of the Pearson Playwrights' Scheme sponsored by Pearson plc.

And our growing number of Individual Supporters

13 Hope Street, Liverpool L1 9BH
www.everymanplayhouse.com
Liverpool Everyman and Playhouse is a registered charity no. 1081229

For Liverpool Everyman and Playhouse

Bank Leumi (UK) is delighted to sponsor Hampstead Theatre and the production of **'3 Sisters On Hope Street'**

With over 100 years of experience working with individuals and companies in the UK, Bank Leumi is a leading provider of Private and Corporate banking services.

Our services include:

- Private Banking
- Trade Finance
- Property Finance
- Israel-Related Finance
- Corporate & Commercial Lending
- Offshore Banking
- Treasury Services

London Office: **020 7907 8008**
Northern Office: **0161 819 4276**
Bank Leumi (Jersey) Limited: **01534 702 525**
www.bankleumi.co.uk

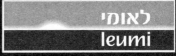

together we go further

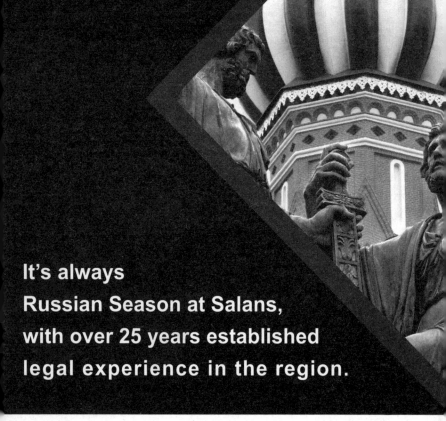

3 SISTERS ON HOPE STREET

Diane Samuels and Tracy-Ann Oberman

after Anton Chekhov

Contents

Authors' Acknowledgements

For their generous, insightful and enthusiastic support, many thanks to:

Gemma Bodinetz at the Liverpool Everyman and Playhouse; Tony Clark and Frances Poet at Hampstead Theatre; Jack Bradley and Lucy Davies at the National Theatre Studio; Sue Andrews; Suzanne Bell; Cecil and Shirley Bredski; Ben Caplan; Luisa Clein; Ruth Corman; Anoushka India Cowan; Robert Cowan; Anna Darvas; Joy Elon; Tom Frederikse; Beil Friend; Peter Gerald; Pascale Giudicelli for French translation; Ilan Goodman; Jeanette Goodman; Mita and Tony Harris; Daniel Hart; Jonathan Hart; David Horovitch; Ian Johnson; Richard Katz; Ivan Kay; Philip Kremen; Belinda Lang; Frank Lazarus; Adam Levy; Shona Morris; David Newman; Isabel Oberman; Michael Parker; Emma Patterson; Chris Pavlo; Dan Rabin; Mark Rosenblatt; Amy Rosenthal; David Rubinger; Helen Samuels; Rubin and Estelle Samuels; Davina Shah; Nitzan Sharron; Sheila Steafel; Micheline Steinberg; Jennie Stoller; Ben Weiner; Wendy Weiner; Susannah Wise and Alexis Zegerman.

Special thanks to Lindsay Posner for script development.

Characters

ARNOLD LASKY, *a brother 'who could have been . . .',*
33 years old, b. 1913

DEBBIE POLLACK, *his fiancée/wife, hungry for it all,*
23 years old, b. 1923

GERTIE LASKY, *eldest sister, weary teacher, spinster and*
mother-figure, 36 years old, b. 1910

MAY (LASKY) FISCHER, *middle sister, married, jaded,*
simmering, 35 years old, b. 1911

RITA LASKY, *youngest sister, baby of the family, budding*
idealist, 25 years old, b. 1921

MORDECHAI 'MORDY' FISCHER, *Hebrew teacher, May's*
husband, pedant, 42 years old, b. 1904

FIRST SERGEANT VINCE SAMUEL, *American flight*
commander, father, distant husband, romantic (from New
Jersey), 42 years old, b. 1904

TEDDY 'TUSH' GOLD, *American air-force clerk, privileged,*
well-educated idealist (from Manhattan, Upper West Side),
29 years old, b. 1917

SOLOMON 'SOLLY' SALZBURGER, *American GI, working*
class, seen the unspeakable, damaged (from Manhattan, the
Bronx), 30 years old, b. 1916

DR NATHAN 'NATE' WEINBERG, *retired gynaecologist,*
lodger, beyond caring, 65 years old, b. 1881

AUNTIE BEIL LASKY, *household fixture, martyr, critic, noch-*
schlepper, 68 years old, b. 1878

OFF-STAGE CHARACTERS (*heard but not seen*)

PETER O'DONNELL, *up-and-coming, Catholic, local*
politician

FREDDY KEANE, *Mr Fix-it*

POTTY POTTER, *unwelcome messenger, harbinger of reality –*
and bills

'OUR BOBBY' LASKY, *Debbie and Arnold's much-beloved*
baby son

Setting

The play takes place in the drawing and dining rooms, a movable partition separating the two, of the Lasky family's house on Hope Street in the centre of the city of Liverpool between 1946 and 1948.

Ideally, the room needs to 'turn' on its axis before and after the interval, offering a different perspective to the audience:

Act One/Act Two – auditorium/audience located beyond the front window of the house looking out onto Hope Street.

Act Three/Act Four – auditorium/audience located beyond back window/doors of house looking out onto garden.

This text went to press before the end of rehearsals and so may differ slightly from the play as performed.

ACT ONE

Sunday, 5th May, 1946.

Early evening.

Inside the house of the Lasky family, Hope Street, near the centre of Liverpool.

The drawing room. Faded grandeur. From the 1920's wireless to the tattered curtains, the elegant edges are fraying and the cracks are showing.

Family photos: a wedding picture of a handsome couple taken in the Edwardian style; separate portraits of three young women and one young man taken in the 1930s.

Most prominent is a photo of a man and woman in early-1920's garb standing on the steps of a New York town house with their four children: a daughter of thirteen, another daughter of twelve, a son of ten and a babe in arms.

GERTIE *is working her way through a pile of exercise books, marking intently.*

MAY *is sitting at the piano, lid closed.*

RITA *is inspecting her birthday cards.*

On a silver tray, a yahrzeit candle, white wax in a small glass, waits to be lit. Beside it is a box of matches and a siddur, prayer book.

MAY *taps the metronome and lets it tick.*

GERTIE *finishes the book she is marking, sighs, goes to the door and calls.*

GERTIE. Arnold!

    Silence.

Arnold!

Silence.

They wait.

ARNOLD *does not come.*

The door opens.

The sisters all look expectantly.

AUNTIE BEIL *enters.*

BEIL. No Arnold?

She turns to go and get him.

GERTIE. Auntie, let him come when he's ready.

BEIL *hovers by the door, just about suppressing the urge to go and get him.*

Can you believe it? A whole year since he died. That was some twenty-fourth birthday, Rita.

Silence.

Never mind, your twenty-fifth'll be better. You look beautiful. You really do. Doesn't she, May?

BEIL. She does.

RITA. I feel quite happy today . . .

GERTIE. A year ago already, and he was just sitting there in his chair, cleaning his pipe.

BEIL. Where's Arnold?

GERTIE. May, you were practising 'Strike Up the Band'. And we were geeing him to sing the harmony at your birthday tea. And you said something about the end of the war nearly here. And he smiled.

RITA. Daddy smiling?

GERTIE. Have we got enough matches?

She opens the box and checks.

We both noticed – didn't we, May? – in the same split second. How grey he was. The way he was twitching.

She opens the box of matches, checks them again, takes out a match to light.

I was desperately trying to remember what Nate might do if he hadn't gone into town. Is that where he is now?

BEIL *sighs and nods.*

All I could do was cradle Daddy in my arms while you were trying to breathe the life back into him. I remember thinking, May, 'All that fuss you kicked up about first-aid training. I knew it would come into its own.'

MAY. But it didn't work.

MAY *stops the metronome.*

GERTIE. And then we pulled the lace tablecloth over him.

BEIL. Is Arnold coming or not?

BEIL *exits in search of* ARNOLD.

GERTIE. Then Nate came back. He was soaking. The heavens had opened. Auntie Beil was mithering him to get the wet coat off his back. But Nate kept clutching his little package of mince like it was gold-dust, kneeling on the floor, dripping all over the show, Auntie running in with towels, trying to mop up. Then she started to howl . . . And that is enough now. It's all over. There won't be any howling today. This is peacetime. There's not a cloud in the sky. And you are going to enjoy your birthday properly this year, my darling.

MAY. Where the hell is Arnold!

MAY *opens the lid of the piano and stabs odd notes.*

Come on, Arnold. Come and light the bloomin' candle!

She plonks on the piano.

GERTIE. D'you really have to do that, May?

MAY. No, I don't have to.

She carries on plonking.

RITA. Take no notice.

GERTIE. We must get this lit before teatime.

RITA. What did Mummy do on our birthdays? Tell me again, Gert.

GERTIE. The very best birthdays were the ones when we lived in New York.

RITA. Were they perfect?

GERTIE. Every year she'd write a song for each of us and serenade us over Special Breakfast in her truest American style . . . with a big, big pile of pancakes and rivers of maple syrup . . . and on my tenth especially I remember the most massive chocolate milkshake . . .

RITA. Oh, I want to go back home to New York more than ever.

MAY *jangles a riff from Gershwin's 'Rhapsody in Blue' on the piano.*

Let's do it. Sell the house. And go home to New York.

MAY. You don't even remember it. You were just a baby.

GERTIE. Wouldn't it be wonderful?

RITA. But what about you, May?

BEIL *makes an entrance.*

MAY. What about dear Arnold?

BEIL *shakes her head.*

RITA. He could easily get a professorship out there.

MAY. God save us from professors.

RITA. And there'll be more clever professors for you, Gertie. You'll have your pick.

GERTIE. May, you could come to visit us every year for the holidays.

MAY. Are we never going to light that candle?

GERTIE *looks to the door.* BEIL *shrugs.* MAY *shrugs.* RITA *shrugs.*

GERTIE *strikes the match. She reads the memorial prayer from the siddur in murmured tones.*

GERTIE. *Yizkor elukim nishmas avi mori Chayim ben Shhmuel sh'helech l'uhlamuh. Ana t'hee naphshuh tzrurah bitzur ha'chayim oot'hee menuchasuh cavood s'vah s'machus es paneychah ne'eemus beeminchah netzach. Amen.*

ALL. *Amen.*

BEIL *rubs her hands together, work to do, and shuffles out of the room.*

MAY *resumes playing 'Rhapsody in Blue'.*

RITA. You know, I think I really can remember our house in Manhattan . . .

GERTIE. Ah, birthday girl . . .

RITA. . . . with the tall, white shutters and Mummy playing to us like this and you teaching me how to dance . . .

GERTIE. Ah, doesn't she look beautiful, May?

RITA. So I've decided . . .

GERTIE *pulls at* RITA *to dance with her.*

GERTIE. Twenty-five today, twenty-five today . . .

MAY *improvises an accompaniment to* RITA *and* GERTIE.

MAY. You're officially on the shelf, love.

GERTIE. . . . She's got the key of the door. She's never been twenty-five before!

GERTIE *hugs* RITA.

They twirl each other.

RITA. No more grey skies.

GERTIE. No more headaches.

RITA. No more grey bread.

GERTIE. No more pesky pupils.

RITA. No more ration books.

GERTIE. Beautiful Rita and May the Irresistible and Arnold the Invincible.

RITA *and* GERTIE. The Laskys are coming to town!!!

    MAY *stops improvising and plays the climactic passage of 'Rhapsody in Blue'.*

GERTIE. Oh, if I'd ever got married I'd have had you play this at my wedding!

RITA. You still might.

GERTIE. Did Auntie Beil say when tea would be ready?

    Voices from outside the window.

TUSH (*offstage*). Give me a break!

    MAY *wolf-whistles* RITA.

GERTIE. Behave yourself!

    MAY *whistles more quietly and seductively.*

    Voices in the hallway, approaching.

SOLLY (*offstage*). One hundred press-ups on each hand builds the same strength as three hundred on both hands . . .

    TUSH *hovers in the doorway, closely followed by* SOLLY.

    TUSH *is the more well-scrubbed of the two, dapper and well-bred.*

SOLLY *is far better-looking but makes much less of his appearance.*

TUSH. Loada bull.

SOLLY. And by going half the speed you double the strength . . .

TUSH. I'm sick of hearing it.

TUSH *comes into the room and makes himself quite at home.*

Are we intruding, ladies?

GERTIE. Never.

SOLLY, *as surreptitiously as he can, takes out a little bottle of aftershave, dabs some onto his hands and face.*

MAY *wrinkles her nose at the smell and wafts it away with a couple of flicks of her hand.*

SOLLY *puts the bottle swiftly back into his pocket.*

TUSH. Is it alright if someone pays a visit today?

GERTIE. Of course.

TUSH *makes himself even more at home.*

RITA. Who?

TUSH. Our new senior officer.

RITA. Sounds ancient.

TUSH. His name is Vince Samuel and he's maybe mid-forties.

RITA. Is he interesting?

SOLLY. He thinks so.

TUSH. Oh, he's a decent enough guy, Sol. Family man. Two daughters back home. Devoted to them. Fruitcake for a wife. The grief she causes him . . .

SOLLY. If that were my old lady. I'd have stopped her mouth on the first whine.

TUSH. . . . Even across the Atlantic, she needs an answer to every little thing. What officer cares whether the drapes match the walls? And every day she wants to know when he's coming home. If I were him, I'd just head east and keep going.

SOLLY *suddenly raises a Communist fist.*

SOLLY. Next posting, Moscow!

TUSH. Ha ha.

NATE WEINBERG *enters, immersed in a two-day old* Evening Express. *He has to squint to read the small print.*

NATE. *Pillow to Post* starring William Prince . . . whoever he is . . . Hmm . . . certificate . . . 'A' . . . At the Majestic . . . Nah . . . Oh . . . Right . . . There's an Edgar Wallace at the Scala . . . *Case of the Frightened Lady* . . . No one does a murder mystery like Mr Wallace . . . Oh . . . *Girl in Chains.* That's more like it. (*To* SOLLY.) And what was I saying to you about Edgar Wallace? Mother came from Liverpool. Father too. Want to put a shilling on it?

RITA. Oh Uncle Nate, not everyone comes from Liverpool.

NATE. Don't they?

RITA *laughs.*

News to me.

RITA *laughs again.*

(*To* SOLLY.) A shilling. (*Holds out his hand.*) Put it here.

RITA *takes his hand and dances* NATE *round the drawing room.*

RITA. Uncle Nate, listen . . .

NATE *takes* RITA *into a waltz, whilst singing Irving Berlin's 'Cheek to Cheek'.*

I've got a plan . . . And not just for me. For all of us . . .

NATE. For all of us, petal?

RITA. To change our lives! Because we've been so starved. And we haven't even realised it.

NATE. Lord heavens, how have we been starving you? Beil! When's tea ready?

RITA. Lying in bed till eleven, doing my hair, filing my nails . . . Even during the war I did nothing. What's the use in that?

NATE. This is terrible. Let the child sleep till lunchtime. And get her a manicure!

RITA. Why am I too good to work, Uncle Nate? Why should I be any different to the docker or tram driver or char scrubbing her doorstep? It's time I got a job.

NATE. Even in a pair of overalls you'd knock 'em dead, my lovely Rita.

RITA. If I am not out of bed every weekday by seven o'clock, just like Daddy, to put in a proper shift, then tip me onto the floor, chuck me out into the street and never let me back in this house ever again.

MAY. Daddy was always up at six. Even at the weekends.

RITA. Even better. Get me up at six.

GERTIE. And is mooching about thinking weighty thoughts one of the positions for which you will be applying?

RITA. I mean it, Gertie.

GERTIE. Your face'll set if you don't watch it.

RITA *sets her serious, 'I mean business' face in stone.*

TUSH. Oh Rita, this craving to work. I understand so well. Heaven save us from privilege.

SOLLY. Heaven save *you*.

TUSH. Believe me, I'm done with the 'good' life.

SOLLY. You don't say?

TUSH. Totally. Since being here I'm appalled by the way my family live. Guess what I was given for my fifth birthday?

SOLLY. A hot-air balloon?

TUSH. A handmade rocking horse . . . of the winner of the Kentucky Derby.

SOLLY. No kidding?

NATE. Really!

TUSH. Life-size. Real horse-hair tail. And mane. My own thoroughbred. And was I happy? Give me a break. I screamed for wheels. God forbid the boy should go without a model version of his father's Cadillac. (*Pause*.) With engine.

SOLLY. My heart bleeds.

SOLLY *laughs towards* RITA. *She looks down. He cuts off his laughter.*

TUSH. And as for the Long Island beach house, a surprise from Pop for their anniversary. Mom takes one look and screams, 'What happened to the swimming pool?' Not even the entire, glorious ocean on our doorstep is enough. And I used to agree with her.

NATE *starts to sing Cole Porter's 'I Get a Kick Out of You' in dulcet tones, not so quietly that he can't be heard.*

I'm telling you, it's not just me who's changing. All the beach houses in the world can't keep back the tidal wave that's coming. The great leveller. Privilege just doesn't wash any more. Everyone had better roll up their sleeves. By the 1960s, I promise, being a worker will be the way of life for every single one of us.

RITA *claps*.

NATE. Not me, my good fellow.

TUSH. You don't count.

SOLLY. You ain't gonna be on this earth much longer, Nate. If a heart attack don't kill ya, rely on me to shoot you in the head.

GERTIE. What a thing to say.

NATE. It's true. What do I do? What have I ever contributed? Apart from reading yesterday's newspaper, what use am I?

He holds out his hand to SOLLY.

Now, lad, what about that shilling you promised to put up?

SOLLY. Look at the sky, old man, and see the cloud.

SOLLY *makes a big 'boom' motion with his arms, like an atomic mushroom.*

TUSH. Is it teatime yet?

The Scouse tones of FREDDY KEANE *waft in from the hallway.*

FREDDY (*offstage*). No, yer alright, Auntie B, I won't stay.

NATE. Aha!

He gets up and disappears out of the room.

RITA. What's he up to?

TUSH. Can't you guess, birthday girl?

RITA. Don't know if I dare.

GERTIE. I do hope that he hasn't gone overboard.

MAY (*to herself*). Whether the weather is cold, or whether the weather is hot, we'll weather the weather . . . whatever the weather . . . weather the weather . . . weather, weather . . .

MAY *lets out an enormous sigh.*

GERTIE. Cheer up, May.

MAY *starts to put on her gloves.*

You're not off, are you? What about the tea? We've pooled all our coupons. We've even got a chocolate cake. Made with fresh eggs. The boys have done us proud.

RITA. Don't go.

MAY. Maybe I'll take a wander round Sefton Park. Or just go home. Happy birthday. Enjoy your tea, honey. Don't mind me . . . Oh, the parties we threw before the war . . . when Daddy was himself. This room got so packed, so hot, so much. I'd even give anything to see fat Mrs Noakes stuff her face with schmaltz herring again. All we've got today is one and a half men and a single candle . . . Oh, take no notice of me. I'll go and feed the ducks . . . then I might get the point of it all.

RITA. Oh May, why do you have to be such a . . . such a . . .

GERTIE. It's alright. I understand.

SOLLY. If a man searches for the meaning of life, that's noble. But if a woman tries, it's plain ugly.

MAY. Shut up, you dreadful man.

He raises his arm in a Nazi salute.

SOLLY. *Sieg Heil.*

They all react in shock.

GERTIE *suddenly utters a gasping sob.*

MAY. Oh, grow up, Gertie.

MAY *starts to adjust her hat onto her head.*

The conversation in the hallway becomes more animated and insistent.

FREDDY (*offstage*). Yer alright, I say, Auntie B.

NATE (*offstage*). Oh, come on, Freddy. Raise a cuppa to our Rita.

FREDDY (*offstage*). Appreciate the invite, like, but for me there's one thing that doesn't go with teatime.

NATE (*offstage*). Sandwiches?

FREDDY (*offstage*). Yanks.

Mutterings of farewell from BEIL, NATE *and* FREDDY.

NATE *sweeps into the room carrying a large object covered in a brightly coloured scarf.*

NATE. Happy birthday, Rita!

GERTIE. Oh my giddy aunt.

TUSH. What did I tell you?

BEIL *pops through the door, shaking her head behind* NATE.

Cautiously, tentatively, RITA *tugs at the scarf and pulls it . . . to reveal a brand new wireless.*

BEIL *shakes her head again, tuts and exits.*

MAY. Nate Weinberg, have you lost your marbles!

NATE. Call me a sentimental old fool. Call me a doting sot.

GERTIE. I'll call you much worse than that.

NATE. Call me whatever you like, precious girl. And what use is a birthday if you can't celebrate in style?

GERTIE. We already have a wireless!

NATE. But this is a new one. The tuning whatsamacallit? . . . knob . . . it works properly. And it's for Rita. So that she can listen to whatever she wants, when she wants. And dance to her heart's content like her darling mother used to dance.

RITA. But how can you possibly afford such a present?

NATE. Afford it! What a thing to ask!

NATE *puts down the new wireless and removes the old one from its spot. He then puts the new one where the old one was and picks up the old one.*

MAY *has sorted her hat and is checking that she has every-thing in her handbag.*

They've forgotten how to treat themselves in this house. And each other. Time we remembered how it's done.

NATE *lugs the old wireless towards the door.*

I'll just put the old one in my room for the time being.

NATE *exits, with wireless.*

BEIL *enters in a fluff.*

BEIL. Are we expecting a commandeer?

TUSH. Must be our new chief.

GERTIE. Don't keep him out in the hall, Auntie.

BEIL. Are you ready for tea yet?

Everyone nods and murmurs extreme readiness for tea.

BEIL *hastens out.*

VINCE SAMUEL *strides in. He is a polite and powerful presence.*

VINCE. My privilege and honour to be here. Vince Samuel.

GERTIE. Welcome. Welcome.

She takes his hand and shakes.

I'm Gertie Lasky.

VINCE. Well now, you must be the eldest.

RITA. And I'm the youngest. Rita. Hello.

VINCE. Hello, ma'am.

They shake hands.

RITA. Delighted to meet you.

VINCE. As am I. Most delighted. But isn't there another sister? I seem to remember Esty and Cyril having three daughters.

GERTIE. You knew our parents!

TUSH. Vince is from New York.

VINCE. New Jersey originally.

RITA. Our mother was a New Yorker born and bred.

MAY. How did you know our parents?

VINCE. Are you the third sister? You must be. Something about your complexion.

MAY's face breaks into a slight smile.

And your smile. Oh, you must be Esty's daughter.

GERTIE. Rita's the one who looks most like Mummy.

RITA. So they say.

MAY holds out her hand.

MAY. I'm May.

VINCE. A real honour, ma'am. You sure have grown, the three of you.

MAY. Have we? Since when?

VINCE. Early twenties?

MAY. We were just kids.

GERTIE. Rita was a babe in arms.

VINCE. We all loved your accents. It was a big family wedding on the Upper West Side. My father was still alive then. Esty's third or fourth cousin? Meyer Samuel.

GERTIE. Meyer Samuel?

VINCE. My mother's Hetty Samuel. Big smoker. Platinum blonde. Five-foot-nothing. Your mom was quite friendly with her. I guess I was nearly twenty when I was introduced to Cyril. He had his eye on a roadster convertible. I was working as a mechanic. He loved cars as much as me.

RITA. You must absolutely adore them then.

VINCE. Still do, ma'am. Almost as much as aeroplanes.

GERTIE. Have you just come here from New York?

RITA. We're moving back there soon, you know.

VINCE. I've been stationed at one of the airbases down in East Anglia, in Norfolk for the last couple of years. So I've been away from home a while. My family live in Brooklyn. Brownsville.

RITA. You must be longing to go back.

VINCE. I sure could do with a decent pastrami on rye and slice of cheesecake.

They all sigh with longing.

MAY. Remember the knishes? Daddy used to take us down to the Lower East Side specially for the knishes there.

VINCE. That would be Yonah Schimmel's.

MAY. Yes! And they had such a choice of fillings. Corned beef. Cabbage. Mushroom. Spinach. Potato.

VINCE. And kasha. Yonnah Schimmel's kasha knishes. Nothing in the world can compare.

MAY. What I wouldn't give for a kasha knish right now.

GERTIE. Hetty Samuel!

MAY. Oh yes. She had a silver cigarette case with her initials on it that she let me open.

VINCE. Solid silver.

GERTIE. I remember. You're the younger son. You have an elder brother?

VINCE. Marty.

GERTIE. Vincent and Marty Samuel. Of course.

MAY. Oh. That was . . . what's-her-name's wedding . . .

GERTIE. Faye Ison, Grossman as was.

MAY. Weren't you the handsome one that everyone was talking about? Weren't there rumours that you were almost engaged to a shiksa?

VINCE. I married her.

GERTIE. Oh.

VINCE. Sadly, a few years later, during the Depression, she died.

GERTIE. Oooh.

VINCE. And then I got married again. To a Yiddishe girl. About ten years ago.

GERTIE. Ah.

VINCE. But in those days, back then, I was in love. Truly in love.

MAY. And you had a moustache, didn't you? A bit like Clark Gable.

VINCE. You do remember.

MAY. Gosh. You've aged so much.

VINCE. A great deal has happened since the early twenties.

GERTIE. At least you're not going grey.

VINCE. I'm way past forty already . . . Say, did you ever walk across the Brooklyn Bridge in the snow? Or even better, in the fog? Of course, there are no bridges quite like that here. But I find some parts of Liverpool, the buildings, to be just like parts of Manhattan. It's the same kinda port. And melting pot. There's that warmth, that wit. Yes, it almost feels exactly the same as New York.

MAY. But it isn't.

VINCE. Still, I would like to come into Liverpool more often. It's more like home than Manchester. I wish that our base at Burtonwood was nearer.

SOLLY. You know why it isn't?

Everyone looks at him.

Because if the base was too near then we wouldn't have to come so far. But it's far. So we're not near.

Silence.

TUSH. Always the wisecracker, hey, Sol.

VINCE. Am I right in thinking your family left New York not long after your mother died?

GERTIE. Daddy couldn't bear it there without her. He was so desperate to come back to Liverpool.

MAY. And to our house and Auntie B.

RITA. I was so little I can't remember a thing.

MAY *starts to weep silently.*

And we've not even been able to visit since we left . . . May?

MAY. Oh, it's nothing.

RITA. You'll set us all off . . .

RITA *starts to become weepy.*

SOLLY *surreptitiously dabs on some more cologne.*

Mummy's buried in New York.

GERTIE. You've never even seen her grave, Rit.

MAY. I can barely remember her face any more. Isn't that terrible? Each one of us will be forgotten too. In the blink of an eye. As if we never happened.

VINCE. You're right. We probably will be forgotten. Or else we'll be remembered in ways no one expects. Time kinda has a way of turning the tables. Wasn't Trotsky the next in line before Lenin died? And now, look at him. Lying in Mexico with a pickaxe through his skull. And that Austrian nudnik, Adolf, banged up in the slammer? They said he'd never catch on. Right! And how long has it taken the British public to turn its back on Churchill? He sure ain't the prime minister any more. But in fifty, sixty years, who knows? Maybe he'll be the greatest Brit that ever lived.

TUSH. And they'll be thanking us for rescuing mankind from a fate worse than hell. And struggling . . .

SOLLY. Blah, blah, blah.

TUSH. Even though we won the war, so many are still having to struggle . . .

BEIL enters to get some tea things. NATE follows behind.

SOLLY. Yah-di-yah-di-yah. Don't give the boy tea and cake, just let him spout another goddam theory.

BEIL. Language, young man!

BEIL exits.

TUSH. Cut it out, Sol. The needle is stuck and we're bored as hell.

SOLLY. Blah-blah-blah.

TUSH. But the shortages, the lack of comforts here . . . they do bring out a kinda spirit in these people.

NATE. Then why do I feel like my shoulders are bowed, my knees are caving in and my life is duller than a silent film?

VINCE. Strengthens character.

GERTIE. This is Vince Samuel from New York, Uncle Nate.

A violin starts to play upstairs. MAY's ears perk up immediately.

NATE. You have to try to convince us that it's good for the soul because otherwise we'd all fall into a fug. And never come out. Ever.

MAY (*listening to the violin from upstairs*). Oh, listen to Arnold.

RITA. He's the most talented of us all.

MAY. Professor Lasky one day, we hope, Daddy hoped . . .

GERTIE's eye twinkles with mischief.

GERTIE. And what about what Arnold hopes?

MAY *and* RITA *burst out laughing*.

RITA. She's coming. She's coming today. I think he's invited her.

MAY. I dread to imagine her latest outfit. If she dares come near this house again wearing anything even remotely like that pink dress with the ferocious frill and hideous red belt then I'm going to have to say something.

GERTIE. May, please . . .

MAY. Some levels of vulgarity, Gertie, are a crime against humanity. And don't pretend that you don't agree with me. I know Arnold. This whole 'interlude' is his bit of fun. Anyway, I heard in Bredski's yesterday that the delightful Miss Pollack is getting up to all sorts with Peter O'Donnell. That jumped-up ass who fancies himself as some kind of bigwig on the council.

GERTIE. But he's Catholic!

MAY. And Arnold is just her nice Jewish boy for her parents on a Friday night.

She sets her hat even more squarely on her head.

GERTIE. You're not still intending to head off, are you, May?

MAY *looks towards the door.*

ARNOLD *enters*.

Well hello, Arnold.

ARNOLD *notices* VINCE.

ARNOLD. Good afternoon.

GERTIE. This is Vince Samuel.

RITA. He's from New York.

GERTIE. And a distant cousin on Mummy's side.

ARNOLD. New York. Good luck, old fellow. My sisters will be all over you like a rash.

VINCE. I'm the one who hasn't given them any peace.

RITA. Look what Arnold made for me for my birthday.

She shows a charcoal portrait on a piece of paper, a lively likeness of her.

'Oh' and other sounds of approval.

ARNOLD. It's just a sketch.

RITA. He's got such a good eye. There's lots more here . . .

She heads towards a pile of various papers.

ARNOLD. Better see what's happening to tea . . .

ARNOLD makes to exit.

MAY and GERTIE both grab hold of him and pull him back into the room.

GERTIE. Don't think that you can escape so easily, lover boy.

ARNOLD. Leave me alone.

MAY. Stop being so coy, you big softie.

GERTIE. Go on, play us a romantic air on your violin.

RITA. Arnold's got a sweetheart! Arnold's got a sweetheart!

NATE grabs ARNOLD by the cheeks and plants a big, fat smacker on his forehead.

NATE. And what is the point of life if not to love!

NATE plants another smacker.

And to love with every ounce of your being!

ARNOLD pushes them all off him.

ARNOLD. Stoppit!

MAY. Aaaah, dearie me, has Arnold lost his rag?

ARNOLD. Arnold is just sick and tired . . . Can't even get a decent night's sleep with all the thoughts buzzing around in my head . . .

MAY. You naughty boy!

ARNOLD. . . . Thoughts about a translation, actually. Of a collection of Russian short stories.

VINCE. You read Russian?

RITA. And French, Spanish, and – don't tell anyone – German.

ARNOLD. Daddy, God rest his soul, made very sure that we were all highly educated. And since he died . . . I've been finding it harder to get down to my studies . . . Just can't concentrate at all . . . I don't know.

MAY. And don't our foreign languages come in so very handy hereabouts?

ARNOLD. Oh, I often pop into our local newsagent and request *'Le journal du jour, s'il vous plait.'*

MAY. You wha'?

They laugh together.

These people have enough trouble with plain English.

VINCE. Try seeing them as lucky people.

MAY. Lucky?

VINCE. To know such educated folk as you. I'll bet that just your being here . . . day by day . . . well, I bet it rubs off. In fifty . . . or I guess . . . maybe a hundred years, who knows how many regular Joes will be . . . what . . . I dunno . . . taking up a musical instrument, turning their hand to a short story or even gassing away in Chinese just because of the Laskys on Hope Street.

MAY takes off her hat.

MAY. I'm staying for tea.

MAY also removes her gloves.

VINCE. I am so glad that I came here.

GERTIE. We all are.

VINCE. This is quite a house. A fine way to live. It's so comfortable. And so many beautiful things. I forgot what a family home can feel like. Not that my family's home is anything like this . . .

TUSH. My pop wasn't always loaded . . . His parents hailed from the shtetl . . . They came over from Poland before he was born . . .

RITA. Daddy came over when he was sixteen from Kishinev. All on his own . . .

VINCE. This sure is the way to live . . . Don't get me wrong . . . I never stop thinking about my two wonderful daughters. And my wife . . . poor woman . . . But if I could just wipe the slate clean . . . I wouldn't get married. Not for any money.

MORDY enters. He is carrying something that looks very much like a book, wrapped in brown paper, bound with string.

MORDY. Happy birthday, *meine scheine Schwegerin.* Here you are.

He proudly hands her the newspaper package.

Are you going to open it now or wait till later?

RITA. Thank you very much, Mordy.

MORDY. My pleasure. My pleasure.

He is clearly desperate for her to open it.

RITA *obliges. She unwraps with care.*

(*To* VINCE.) May I introduce myself? Mordechai Fischer, MA.

GERTIE. Mordy is deputy headmaster at our local Jewish junior school.

MORDY. On Hope Place. Up the road and second on the left. Next door to the shul, as was. The congregation from there was displaced just before the war. They've mostly been absorbed into the rather snazzier shul on Greenbank Drive.

But I have to admit that I was rather partial to making up a minion on Hope Place. Still. What can you do?

VINCE. First Sergeant Vincent Samuel. Third cousin to Esty Lasky. Pleased to meet you.

MORDY. Likewise.

RITA *has opened her package. She looks inside the sombre, dark blue cover of the book.*

RITA. Didn't you give me this Authorised Daily Prayer Book for my birthday last year?

MORDY. No, no, no. Last year I gave you a quite different Authorised Daily Prayer Book, Rita. But we're very fortunate that Dr J.H. Hertz, as you know our Chief Rabbi as was, *olev hashalom*, has now very recently published an edition with a very well laid out commentary which I personally find more than a little edifying. And I do hope that you will too.

RITA. So there's a rabbinical commentary on every prayer?

MORDY. On every page.

MAY. I bet you can't wait a second more to get stuck in?

MORDY. Ah, beloved wife!

He kisses MAY.

Show the commentary to First Sergeant Samuel, Rita. I'm sure he'll find it very interesting.

RITA *closes the book.*

RITA. Not now.

A general sigh permeates the room.

MORDY. Sunday afternoon lethargy seems to have set in. And what's wrong with that? We all need to wind down. Isn't that what the weekend's for?

He lets his gaze dwell on the yahrzeit candle.

Ah, Cyril. I wish you all 'long life', girls, and you too,
Arnold. Yes, a low-key celebration is very much in order.
Now, Rita, I recommend that you wind up the piece of string
before you forget and fold up the paper for re-use. Waste not,
want not. Paper doesn't grow on trees . . . Paper. From trees.
Ha ha . . . Oh well . . . Oh yes . . . You should have heard
Reverend Pearl when some of the children in cheder were
playing catch with an apple. 'Have more respect for food,' he
tells them. 'Apples don't grow on trees!' And the children
realised what he'd said before he did. They were hooting
with laughter. 'Apples don't grow on trees!' . . .

GERTIE. Apples don't grow on trees!

MORDY. May, we're invited over to the Pearls' this evening for
dinner at seven o'clock.

MAY. I can't go.

MORDY. But I heard they might have a chicken!

MAY. I can't go!

MORDY. But after dinner, there's a game of rummy with the
Raismans!

MAY. Oh, for Pete's sake . . . Alright . . . Just stop going on
about it.

MORDY (*to* VINCE). See, how my wife loves me.

BEIL *enters with a chipped teacup and silver teaspoon. She
taps the spoon against the cup.*

BEIL. Teatime!

ARNOLD, TUSH *and* MORDY *help push back the partition
to reveal a laid table with sandwiches, biscuits and cakes,
more abundant than post-war austerity normally allows.*

*Everyone 'Oohs' appreciatively and declares 'What a feast!',
'This is incredible!'*

GERTIE. Well, thanks to our American friends, we've gone
to town!

Everyone applauds the tea.

The sandwiches are fresh. And guess what? There's tinned salmon.

More 'Oohs'.

And we even got some cream cheese. So sorry. We tried, but we couldn't find full-fat anywhere.

Everyone sighs.

But there are some cucumber slices in those. And some egg and cress.

Everyone cheers.

TUSH. Try the peanut butter and jelly. What d'you call it?

MORDY. Jam.

TUSH. And we brought the dried fruit. Try the prunes.

Everyone 'Mmmms'.

SOLLY. Try the chocolate drops.

BEIL. Sit down. Sit down. Try some herring. Help yourselves. And let me pour you some tea, flight commandeer.

VINCE. Thank you so much.

MORDY. I was good for nothing yesterday. I've never had so much marking in my life.

GERTIE. You were up far too late with it on Thursday. You looked so drawn on Friday at school assembly. I'm glad to see you've got a bit more of your colour back, Mordechai.

MORDY. Do you think I'd be more impressive if I grew a moustache? I'm quite taken with the one Reverend Pearl sports. He models it on Mr Attlee, you know.

GERTIE. Would May like that?

MAY. No, May would not like that.

BEIL. Arnold, see the bottle there. Offer the flight commandeer a drop of Scotch.

NATE *emerges from a quick shufty at his newspaper.*

NATE. Did someone say . . . egg and cress? Yes, we're really celebrating in top style.

MAY. And don't think that you're going to top it off with any of the hard stuff.

NATE. When did you last see me on the bottle? It's been ages. Years. A lifetime.

MAY. Keep it that way, you old renegade.

NATE. Aye, aye, your ladyship.

NATE *salutes her.*

MAY. Not a drop, Nathan Weinberg. I mean it. I'll be keeping an eye on you all evening . . . Oh hell. Reverend Pearls of Wisdom . . .

TUSH. So don't get dragged to the Rabbi's, May. Stick around here with us.

NATE. Find a way to get out of it.

MAY. I've only gone and bloody agreed now, haven't I! Bloody hell!

NATE. Cheer up, May. At least you'll get a roast bird.

MAY *and* NATE *join the rest at table.*

SOLLY. Blah-di-blah-di-blah.

TUSH. Have you still not got the message? Zip it.

SOLLY. Blah-di-blah.

MORDY *raises his teacup to* VINCE.

MORDY. Cheers to our American cousins. I hope I may call you that. Technically, it's accurate, since I am related through my darling wife May.

VINCE. How about a toast with this fine whisky? (*He toasts*.) Happy birthday, Rita. *Le'chayim!* This is such a privilege. I mean it. Home from home.

RITA *goes into the living room to get some more glasses*.

TUSH *comes to help her*.

RITA. May is being a right sourpuss. I suppose I shouldn't blame her. I'd probably be the same after eight years of marriage to the deputy head. He was a deputy, you know, before he was even appointed. I think that he was even a deputy when he was born. Before he was born.

TUSH. Is that the only thing on your mind?

RITA. What's wrong with Solly?

TUSH. You kinda get used to the cheap cologne after a while.

They both grimace at the thought.

RITA. But why's he like that all the time? He scares me.

TUSH. He isn't always like that. We get on better when it's just the two of us. He's more relaxed. He understands a lot more than you can tell. He reads all the time. I guess he just finds it hard in company. He's been through some tough stuff.

RITA. Tell me.

TUSH. He was one of the guys that liberated Dachau.

RITA *stares at* SOLLY.

You're twenty-five and life is going to get better and better for you. Just looking at you makes me believe that my life is going to get better too. I hope that we can spend even more time together. Just us. I mean it, when I say . . . I mean it that I love you . . .

RITA. Teddy, please.

TUSH. Don't you agree that we want the same things?

RITA. Do we?

TUSH. Come on. We want to build the same kind of world. I know we do. Beautiful Rita, so full of passion. You inspire me to be a man of action, to make things happen. Not just to say, 'Next year in Jerusalem.' We can do it, you and me.

RITA. Jerusalem seems so far away. Even further than New York.

She starts to cry and turns her head away.

TUSH. It's okay.

RITA. Look at me. I am so useless. My grandparents . . . I never even knew them . . . used to work like dogs. But it didn't get them very far in the old country. Thank God Daddy got out. And Auntie B. They struggled so we didn't have to. 'No pogroms over here. Vaht more could you vant?' We're the lucky ones. We're alive. We're so terribly comfortable. But, Teddy, why do I still wonder where I belong? It's so silly.

TUSH. It's not silly. How can any Jew feel safe in Europe ever again?

A head pokes round the door.

It belongs to DEBBIE POLLACK.

DEBBIE. Am I too late to wish you a very happy birthday, Rita?

RITA. Well, we've started tea already.

DEBBIE. I brought you a little something.

DEBBIE *enters and holds out a parcel of newspaper.*

She is wearing a pink dress with a frill at the neck and a red belt. Her shoes are also red.

RITA *takes the package. There are stains on the paper.*

RITA. Oh, is this blood?

DEBBIE. Oh sorry. It's from Dad's shop. Something special. No coupons needed. (*She nods a wink.*) I hope you like steak.

RITA. Gosh. Well, that is a treat. Thank you so much.

RITA *goes off to put away the steak.*

MAY *laughs out loud in response to something* VINCE *has said to her.*

GERTIE *glances at* VINCE *and* MAY. *She rises to greet* DEBBIE.

GERTIE. Are you joining us, Debbie?

DEBBIE. Is it terrible that I'm so late? And you've got so many visitors.

GERTIE. Oh, we don't stand on ceremony here. (*She pulls* DEBBIE *aside*.) But a word to the wise. That belt. It's really rather . . . You might want to take it off. Before someone says something.

DEBBIE. Oh. Why? What's wrong with it?

GERTIE *shakes her head then finds* DEBBIE *a place at table.*

DEBBIE *tries surreptitiously to adjust her dress over her belt as she sits.*

Gosh, where d'you get all this from?

GERTIE. Just help yourself, dear.

MORDY. Well, Rita, now you're advancing in years I hope that soon you'll be settling down with someone suitable.

NATE. And may Miss Pollack find someone suitable too.

MORDY. Does Miss Pollack not already have a suitor?

MAY. A drop more tea, Arnold. And make it strong.

He pours into her cup.

And even stronger.

She drops a dash of whisky into her tea.

MORDY. C-minus, May Fischer, for misconduct.

VINCE. These fish balls are delicious.

BEIL. Thanks to Wing Admiral Salzburger.

RITA. You know Solly's in the army, Auntie.

SOLLY. I gutted the fish myself. And chopped off their heads.

RITA. Ugh, don't be so disgusting.

GERTIE. Auntie B, are you ready?

BEIL. Ready, ready.

BEIL *bustles out.*

GERTIE. Vince, do you like potato kugel?

VINCE. I love it nearly as much as latkes.

GERTIE. Well, maybe one Friday night we'll splash out and provide both for you.

VINCE. Would this Friday be too soon?

RITA. We'll hold you to that.

DEBBIE. That's an awful lot of potatoes.

NATE. Well, of course, some of us would rather have a private dinner for two rather than a family feast, wouldn't you, my dear?

ARNOLD. That is enough!

BEIL *enters holding a birthday cake with a single candle burning.*

GERTIE *starts singing the 'Happy Birthday' refrain. Everyone joins in.*

RITA *blows out the candle.*

ARNOLD *starts up singing 'For She's a Jolly Good Fellow'.*

NATE *sings this very loudly and at the climax of the song he pulls out of his pocket a handful of boiled sweets and showers them over* RITA.

RITA (*delighted*). Pear drops!

NATE. Enjoy, everyone.

MAY. . . . We'll weather the weather whatever the weather . . . Oh, I just can't get that blessed thing out of my head.

ARNOLD *passes a sweetie to* DEBBIE.

NATE. Sweets for his sweetheart, I see.

DEBBIE *flushes*.

My dear girl, you've gone as red as your belt.

Everyone laughs.

DEBBIE *runs away from the table*.

ARNOLD *follows and pulls the partition to give them some privacy*.

ARNOLD. Oh, *ma petite. Ma petite*, take no notice. Just ignore them.

DEBBIE. Now I've made an even bigger idiot of myself by leaving table. Why am I such a laughing stock, Arnold? Why?

ARNOLD. It's not just you. I promise, darling. They give me an even harder time.

DEBBIE. But you're all so grand and clever. I haven't a clue what your sisters are on about half the time.

ARNOLD. It's just teasing. You'll get used to it. No harm is meant. It's all done in love. Part of being so close. It means that you're one of us.

DEBBIE. It doesn't feel like it.

ARNOLD. You'll get used to it. Trust me. You're family now, *ma petite chere*.

DEBBIE. I find it all a bit much. I'm sorry.

He kisses her tenderly.

ARNOLD. And this is why I love you, Debbie Pollack. Because you don't go in for airs and graces. You're just yourself. You make me happy. So happy. Let them tease all they like. We have each other. Please keep on making me happy. Debbie, will you marry me?

Pause.

DEBBIE. Oh Arnold, can you say it in French?

ARNOLD. *Je t'aime, Debbie Pollack, épouse-moi!*

DEBBIE *pulls him to her and kisses him passionately.*

ACT TWO

Saturday, 29th March, 1947.

Early afternoon.

The drawing room. The 'new' wireless is positioned in a focal point with chairs set around it.

The room has been spruced up a little, the furniture has been moved around slightly, some chintzier ornaments have appeared.

A wedding photo of DEBBIE *and* ARNOLD *has pride of place. The other family photos are now more in the background.*

DEBBIE *enters with a muslin over her shoulder, doing up the buttons of her bright yellow blouse. She sighs when she sees the wireless, chairs around it and the piano lid open, sheets of music strewn.*

DEBBIE. Arnold!

She closes the piano lid and packs the music away in the stool.

Arnold!

DEBBIE *tuts and straightens up the room some more.*

ARNOLD *enters, carrying a book.*

ARNOLD. Did you call?

DEBBIE. Where were you?

ARNOLD. Just reading.

DEBBIE. Honestly, Arnold. You promised. Straight after lunch, you swore to me that you'd make up the fire in Bobby's room.

ARNOLD. Auntie Beil said she'd do that.

DEBBIE. Well, I can't find Auntie Beil.

ARNOLD. She must have gone down to the bookie's with Nate.

DEBBIE. Oh.

ARNOLD. She'll do it as soon as she gets back.

DEBBIE. But we're freezing our socks off.

ARNOLD. Gertie did mention that we're running low again and to be careful with the coal . . .

DEBBIE. Oh, but that doesn't apply to the baby.

ARNOLD. Shall I go and make up a little fire then?

DEBBIE. Bobby's in there sleeping now. I had to put two extra blankets on him. This house really is cold as the grave.

ARNOLD. A little bit of spring chill won't harm him. He's a hearty lad, Deb.

ARNOLD *wheezes slightly.*

DEBBIE. I just hope that the two blankets are enough, poor little sausage. You saw how flushed he was yesterday. And now he's gone to ice. You don't think he's got pneumonia, do you?

ARNOLD. He seemed alright to me.

DEBBIE. But he was so fretful in the night . . . I'm sure he's brewing something, Arnold.

ARNOLD. Let Nate take a look at him then.

DEBBIE. He's not the right kind of doctor at all . . . Not for a little baby.

ARNOLD. He's very compassionate and clever. He knows what he's doing.

DEBBIE. If you're a girl in trouble I'm sure that's right.

Silence.

ARNOLD. Well, I don't know about any of that. I really don't.

Silence.

Look, just don't worry so much about Bobby, *ma cherie*.
He's doing fine.

DEBBIE. And I do hope that he's not going to be disturbed later.

ARNOLD. Why should he be?

DEBBIE. How many people are meant to be coming round?

ARNOLD. Oh, just the usual.

DEBBIE. Gertie's not back yet, either, is she?

ARNOLD. Isn't she?

DEBBIE. She could have told me that she was going for lunch
at the Karp's after shul. At least I saw Rita this morning.
D'you know what time she left? Seven thirty. On a shabbos.
She could do a lot better, you know, Arnold, now that she's
got all her qualifications sorted. She's worth more than
slaving for some shyster goyshe accountant on London
Road. You should have a word with her.

ARNOLD. Yes, yes. I'll have a quiet chat after the race.

DEBBIE *pulls a face*.

Are you alright, darling?

DEBBIE. I'm just not sure, Arnie. Not today. Bobby's barely a
month old. Isn't it a bit soon for all and sundry to be making
a right old rumpus in our drawing room? Can't you call it
off, darling? Please?

ARNOLD. But it's the Grand National.

DEBBIE. They can still put their money on and everything. It
won't spoil their fun. And I'm sure that Bobby's aunties will
understand. They love him as much as we do.

ARNOLD. Of course they do. They adore him.

DEBBIE. D'you really think so?

ARNOLD. I'm sure they'd cut off their right arms for him.

DEBBIE. Well, d'you think Rita might let him move into her room? It's warmer there. And she could share with Gertie until summer. Just for a couple of months.

ARNOLD *is very silent. He stares blankly at his book.*

What d'you think, Arnold?

ARNOLD. Well . . . I mean . . .

The doorbell rings.

ARNOLD *coughs and pats his chest as if trying to clear it.*

DEBBIE. Please, Arnold? Ask Rita.

The doorbell rings again.

For Bobby's sake?

DEBBIE *gives him a little kiss.*

ARNOLD. I'll have to have a little think about it . . .

ARNOLD *puts down his book and hastens out to get the door.*

DEBBIE *starts to move the chairs back. She also keeps an ear open for the conversation that ensues in the hallway.*

(*Offstage.*) Hello, Potter.

POTTER (*offstage*). Files from Mr O'Donnell. Council business.

ARNOLD (*offstage*). You could have waited till Monday morning.

POTTER (*offstage*). It's urgent, Mr Lasky.

ARNOLD (*offstage*). And which horse have you got your eye on for this afternoon?

POTTER (*offstage*). My money's on Wish Me Luck.

ARNOLD (*offstage*). Well then, Potter, I wish you luck.

POTTER (*offstage*). Wish me wha'?

ARNOLD (*offstage*). Luck!

Sounds of goodbyes.

ARNOLD *enters the living room carrying a folder filled with papers.*

Look what I've let myself in for, agreeing to do that report on city reconstruction for the council. Ridiculous facts and figures. Load of made-up propaganda. I've never met a bunch who scratch each others backs like this lot.

DEBBIE *has picked up the book he left lying around and holds it out to him.*

When am I going to have time to catch up on my Proust for my PhD?

DEBBIE. Will you just help me shift the wireless back to where it belongs?

ARNOLD. But Debbie, you need to ask Gertie and Rita at least . . .

Crying from upstairs.

DEBBIE. Oh heck.

ARNOLD. His lungs sound hearty enough to me.

DEBBIE. Please, Arnold, just move the wireless for us. And make up a fire in the morning room too.

DEBBIE *dashes out to see to* BOBBY.

I'm coming, our Bobby!

ARNOLD *weighs the file heavily in his hand and opens the book then closes it.*

The crying continues.

ARNOLD *listens for a moment, then sighs and leaves the room.*

Silence.

Upstairs a violin starts to play.

The crying starts to recede.

Voices in the hallway.

MAY *enters. She is carrying a basket of bottles of drinks.*

MAY. No, there's no one here yet.

VINCE *enters. He is carrying a box.*

What time is it?

VINCE *indicates that he can't look at his wristwatch whilst holding the box.*

VINCE. You tell me.

MAY *laughs. She contorts herself to see his watch. This involves having to take his hand and move it to make the watch face clearly visible.*

MAY. Better get set up.

MAY *and* VINCE *unpack their goodies.* MAY *takes charge, finding bowls for the sweets, chocolate, nuts that* VINCE *has brought. She has bottles of lemonade, ginger beer, a whisky and a vodka.*

Thank you so much for all this nosh. What a splendid treat.

VINCE. Well, that's why we guys came over here, to save you from misery.

MAY. And a very good job you're doing too.

VINCE. My personal pleasure, ma'am.

MAY. Hey, can I show you something?

VINCE. Please do.

MAY *digs around in a cupboard.*

MAY. Rita and I found these the other day. We thought Gertie had thrown them away.

She shows VINCE *a bowl of metal pieces, one is much larger than the rest.*

VINCE. You keep shrapnel?

MAY. During the war, even before the all-clear sounded, Rita, Arnold and I would run up from the cellar out into the streets and collect it. Our very own trophies of war. Like a bunch of kids, we were. But this one . . .

She almost strokes the largest piece.

This beauty came to us.

VINCE. Aaah, the boarded window upstairs.

MAY. From the house over the road. You could have heard the explosion in Wallasey. It's a miracle that all our windows weren't shattered.

VINCE. There were a lot of miracles during the war.

MAY. Is that the case?

VINCE. You're looking at one.

MAY. So you're a miraculous man, are you?

VINCE. By rights I should not be standing here with you now.

MAY. And why are you?

VINCE *shrugs*. MAY *shrugs*.

So why are you here?

VINCE. I can't recall the number of times I faced the flak coming so thick you could walk on it. But like your house, I came out with no more than a clipped wing. And yet so many buddies of mine, fine pilots, were shot down when there wasn't an enemy aircraft in sight.

MAY. You have something in common then with Auntie Beil.

VINCE. Me and Auntie B?

MAY. She was fast asleep when the shrapnel shattered her window. And this fellow . . . (*She wields the largest piece.*) landed smack-bang on the floor, inches from her head.

Cross my heart, there was not a scratch upon her. And she just pulled back the sheets, dragged her suitcase from under the bed . . .

VINCE. Was she planning on taking a trip?

MAY. Oh, that suitcase came with her from Russia. She always has it packed in case she needs to make a hasty exit. 'If you've got a spare pair of shoes, you can always run.' And she keeps her passport under her pillow.

VINCE. Well, the wind can always turn.

MAY. And the night the shrapnel landed it did turn. But she didn't have to escape too far this time. She just grabbed her passport, took herself off to the boxroom, then went straight back to sleep.

VINCE. And she's still in there?

MAY. With the suitcase forever packed under her bed.

VINCE. You should get that broken window replaced.

MAY. Yes, we should.

VINCE *takes the shrapnel and gets the feel of it.*

You've probably encountered bigger and nastier brutes than this little guy.

VINCE. Tell the truth, no bullet, no missile, no atomic bomb compares to the bombardment coming my way from the other side of the Atlantic.

MAY. I might complain too if you were my husband and so far away for so long.

VINCE. But your complaints are so much more entertaining, May. I might even find myself looking forward to them.

MAY. Unlike my husband who hardly seems to notice.

VINCE. But he's so devoted to you.

MAY. Aren't I the lucky little Eshet Chayil.

VINCE. I often imagine what my life would be like without her.

MAY. I often imagine what your conversation would be like without her. She's all you talk about.

VINCE (*laughs*). You're right. I'm like a dog gnawing on a sucked-out bone.

MAY. I wouldn't mind a little gnaw myself. Is any of that choccie going yet?

VINCE *breaks off a piece from his goodie supply and holds it out to her mouth.*

MAY *slowly, carefully, takes it between her lips and sucks.*

Mmmmm.

VINCE *'Mmmms' as well. There is a moment, too long, and then . . . he abruptly stiffens.*

VINCE. Ah, but when I was called to the telephone this morning . . . for the third time for chrissakes . . . And she was still . . .

MAY. Enough is enough! You're obsessed!

MAY *turns on the wireless and fiddles with the knob till she finds some music.*

Bing Crosby is singing 'Swinging on a Star'. MAY *starts to join in, followed by* VINCE.

They shift the wireless even more into pride of place and put the chairs around it. MAY *starts swinging provocatively as she sets the room, singing throughout.*

VINCE. Oh, you . . . you . . . the way you move . . .

MAY *moves some more. And some more.*

You . . . sensational . . . phenomenal . . . You ravishing woman . . . I adore you . . .

MAY. Stoppit, you schmoozer.

VINCE *stares at her silently.*

What? Why have you gone so quiet?

VINCE. I totally adore you.

The door bursts open and RITA *enters, still wearing her coat, in a flourish of exasperation and heightened exhaustion. She flops into the biggest armchair.*

MAY *turns down the volume on the wireless.*

VINCE *attends to the furniture.*

TUSH *enters. He is carrying* RITA*'s handbag and a couple of brown paper bags.*

RITA. I don't even have the energy to take off my coat.

TUSH. I am so proud of you, Rita, for finishing your first week.

RITA. Stop saying that. I heard you the first time.

TUSH. I'll keep saying it till you feel proud too.

RITA. How can I feel proud when they keep giving me the awful chores like making the teas and changing the ink ribbons and tidying out the stationery cupboard? Did I train at Miss Foulkes to become a dogsbody?

MAY. Flash your eyelashes at the boss, Rita. (*To* VINCE.) You couldn't get us some more mascara, could you?

VINCE *nods and smiles.*

RITA. I suppose he is rather dishy.

MAY. Is he? Your boss? Tell more.

TUSH. I thought you wanted to be respected as a professional.

RITA. I do.

TUSH. Then behave like one and you'll be given the work you're qualified for.

RITA. I am trying.

RITA *lets out a whimper.*

MAY. Oh, poor little kitten.

RITA whimpers some more.

I swear that in just the last seven days you've got thinner.

RITA. It's non-stop. A million little jobs at a time. And not one of them means a thing.

MAY. At this rate you'll be skin and bone by Pesach.

RITA. I never wanted to work for an accountant anyway. I want to do something worthwhile. I'd much rather get a job at the children's hospital. I could work in the offices there . . . They must need people with my skills, surely. And then in some way I'll be helping the poor, little sick children. At least there's some point to that.

MAY. What's the time now?

MAY takes VINCE's wrist and looks at his watch.

TUSH. Time to tune in?

TUSH goes to the wireless and starts turning the knob.

Sounds of voices, NATE and BEIL, in the hallway.

NATE (*offstage*). Next year we should definitely try to go to Aintree, I say. I'll buy you a new hat for the occasion.

Sounds of BEIL muttering about hats and schnapps.

MAY. Do you know how much Arnold's putting on today?

RITA. I hope it's not much. Not after his losses on Wednesday night.

MAY. Did he go with Nate to that poker game again?

RITA sighs and nods.

Just don't let the Big Mama know what's going on.

NATE enters, immersed in the newspaper and sorting through various bits of paper.

And what about the rent?

NATE *becomes even more immersed in the bits of paper.*

RITA. He's forgotten what the word means.

MAY. Since when?

RITA. Oh, I don't know. Probably since we won the war.

MAY. We won the war? News to me.

TUSH. I think you'll find that we did win it, ma'am.

MAY. Which is why bread is now being rationed. But hey, that's how it goes for winners. They run short of everything.

TUSH. It could be a lot worse.

MAY. Put that by me again.

TUSH. It could be a lot, lot worse.

MAY. What about it actually being better?

RITA sighs an even more enormous sigh than before.

NATE has now sorted his betting slips.

NATE. I do hope that I've got this right.

He checks and hands a slip to RITA.

Rita, Prince Regent. Yes? The favourite gets the favourite.

BEIL enters with a bottle of schnapps and a newspaper.

BEIL. I knew we had some schnapps left over from the briss.

RITA. Wasn't Debbie saving that for the next special occasion?

BEIL. This is the next special occasion.

She puts the schnapps down on the table.

NATE checks the next betting slip and passes it to MAY.

NATE. May, my dear, Lovely Cottage has been withdrawn, so I took the liberty of taking a punt on Black Jennefer for you. You being the dark horse of the family.

RITA *glances at* MAY *nervously.*

It's all just a bit of fun, just a bit of fun.

BEIL. Black Jennefer, you say?

She squints intently at her newspaper, searching through the list of horses.

VINCE *glances at the list over her shoulder.*

NATE *waves a third slip.*

NATE. And for sister number three, we have the outsider, Caughoo.

RITA. Where is Gertie?

BEIL. Caughoo?

MAY. She went for lunch after shul to the Karp's with Mordy.

VINCE helpfully points down the list for BEIL.

VINCE. Caughoo.

BEIL. Ahh. Caughoo.

NATE. And for Arnold, we have Domino, Fallen and Kami.

RITA. Three horses!

NATE. His choices, not mine.

BEIL. Domino. Did he say Domino?

VINCE points again on the name in the list.

RITA. It's not fair Arnold gets three horses.

MAY. How much has he put on them, Nate?

NATE taps his nose conspiratorially with his finger.

NATE. And for Mrs Arnold Lasky, nee Pollack, I took the further liberty of selecting Prattle.

Everyone hoots with laughter.

RITA. Who have you got, Uncle Nate?

NATE. A little birdie told me to go for Gyppo.

BEIL. What? Who?

VINCE. Gyppo, Beil.

BEIL. Gyppo?

VINCE. There. See.

VINCE *helpfully points out the horse in the paper.*

BEIL. Yes, but Gyppo likes the going firm to hard. And today it's heavy. Take my word, Gyppo'll fall at Beechers, if not the first time round, then the second.

NATE. What do you know?

MAY *and* RITA. What doesn't she know!

BEIL. What don't I know!

NATE. Go and get us a cup of tea, old woman.

VINCE (*imitating an English accent*). I could kill for a cup of tea.

BEIL. I'm studying the form. Gyppo! Ach. My Gertie's got her money on the nose. An outsider will take it today. But don't listen to me. What do I know? Have a schnapps.

BEIL *returns to her paper.*

RITA *offers round glasses. When she reaches* NATE *she pauses.*

MAY *throws a warning glance.*

NATE *makes a big show of refusing the glass anyway.*

NATE. So . . . The Scotsman says, 'I'm thirsty, I must have whisky.'

MAY. Is that right, Mr *Wine*-berg?

TUSH *opens the schnapps and pours a little for everyone. He makes a careful display of not giving any to* NATE.

NATE. The Irishman says, 'I'm thirsty, I must have Guinness.'

The Englishman says, 'I'm thirsty, I must have beer.'

And the Jew says, 'I'm thirsty . . . I must have . . . diabetes.'

Everyone laughs.

VINCE *raises his glass.*

VINCE. To diabetes!

ALL. Diabetes!

All but NATE *drink.*

RITA. How long before the big race? It had better start before I drop off.

TUSH *cocks an ear to the wireless and looks at his watch.*

TUSH. Long enough to chew the fat.

He turns down the volume.

MAY. Rita's not the only one who'll drop off if you start one of your Big Discussions.

RITA. That's the one thing that'll keep me awake. I find them interesting.

MAY. Since when?

RITA. Since forever.

MAY *raises her eyebrows.*

So does NATE.

VINCE. So have you thought any more about where our future lies, Tush?

TUSH. I've been chewing on it, sure.

RITA. Will you all be going back to New York soon?

MAY. Back to New York with the guys? What d'you reckon, Rita?

TUSH. It's not as simple as that . . .

MAY. But if we wait any longer we'll shrivel to nothing.

TUSH. If we wait any longer, you're right, we will shrivel to
nothing. But I'm not talking about going back. The real work
is not in New York.

MAY *sighs – half-mocking, half-serious – and closes her
eyes, covers her ears.*

You have a problem with what I'm saying?

RITA. Take no notice.

TUSH. May, none of us can avoid it any more. Read Herzl.

NATE. Ah, the Jewish question.

MAY. Is there only one?

VINCE. Where do I truly belong?

MAY. Right here with us.

RITA. What about with your family in Brooklyn?

TUSH. Where do any of us belong? Where is the heart of our
nation when we're so scattered? And now so depleted.

NATE. So we're a nation, are we? No longer simply a people.
Just people. Ordinary people. Impossible people . . .

TUSH. A people always in the minority. There is not one state
in the entire world where our interests matter. The most we
are ever allowed to be is welcome guests. If we behave ourselves. And even then they can turn on us overnight.

NATE. Ah, the eternal Jewish question.

TUSH. To which there is only one viable solution.

NATE. But what Jew is ever happy with a solution? No sooner
you find one, you're looking for the next problem.

TUSH. We need our own state.

NATE (*singing*). In our Liverpool home . . .

MAY. We Laskys just need to go to New York where we belong.

TUSH. New York is not Zion. It is not our home.

MAY. You might long for the sand between your toes, but the shopping's a darn sight better on Fifth Avenue.

RITA *laughs with relish*.

TUSH. Give me a shovel and I'll build you shops beyond your wildest dreams in the wilderness. And I'll build schools. And hospitals. And orchards of oranges, olives, pomegranates . . . You name the fruit, I'll make the desert bloom for you, Rita.

RITA *claps*.

VINCE. Things can't be solved just like that.

TUSH. They can. Sooner than any of us dare believe.

RITA. Really? How soon?

VINCE. It'll take much longer than you think.

TUSH. But Vince, I tell you again, we can't afford for it to take any longer.

VINCE. So, what if our very own state is established tomorrow? You think all our problems end there?

TUSH. Our new life begins. A brighter future becomes a bright present. No more 'Next year in Jerusalem.' We can say, 'This year. We are here. This is now.'

VINCE. You've never been to Jerusalem . . . It's not a simple place . . . How do I explain? It's these different worlds rubbing against each other . . . Chassidim walking around like they own the place, dressed like they're in some eighteenth-century Polish shtetl. Arabs in kaffiyahs on mules who look like they grew out of the rock itself . . . British soldiers in khaki shorts mopping their brows every five seconds. And they all claim, 'This land is mine.'

RITA. Have you been there?

VINCE. Yeah, I've been there.

MAY. You never said.

VINCE. I was in my twenties. A kid. I guess I was lost, looking for a place to settle. Or else I was trying to escape.

MAY. Was this after your first wife died?

VINCE. That's right. The 'shiksa' died. So I went to the Land of My Fathers.

RITA. Why didn't you settle there?

VINCE. Pop got sick. I had to go back to New York. The more places I've been, the more battles I've fought, the more I realise that we are not the guys who are going to get to the Promised Land . . .

TUSH. Try telling that to those desperate refugees shipped to Cyprus by the Brits. For God's sake, haven't these guys seen enough barbed wire? We all gotta fight so they can at last come home.

VINCE. That fight you're seeking ain't gonna be quick. The Arabs see us overrunning their homeland. You think they'll put up with us being in charge? And why the hell should they? So is it us or is it them? Cos this sure as hell ain't a marriage made in heaven. A hard battle lies ahead. And we can only hope that our children . . . our children's children . . . their children after them . . . will be the ones who get to be happy and safe and settled. But we can't expect that. Not for ourselves. We just have to struggle. Like cousin Yitz used to say out in the field, 'Keep on pushing these boulders of hope up mountain of our dreams, comrade.'

MAY *laughs*.

TUSH. What's so funny?

MAY. I just feel rather happy today for some reason.

VINCE. You really dare to be happy in such hard times, May?

MAY. I dare.

VINCE. And what if you're just kidding yourself?

MAY. And what if you're more than a mule pushing boulders up a mountain?

(Singing.) Or would you rather be a pig?

VINCE *laughs*.

MAY *laughs*.

TUSH. We must have a home. Now.

SOLLY *enters. He is patting his face, just finishing off the latest application of aftershave.*

BEIL. Ach. The Cossacks'll come after us wherever we are.

Various protests and sympathies with BEIL's comment.

BEIL *goes up to the radio and puts her ear close.*

Is it the 2.30?

NATE. Shhh.

NATE *rattles the JNF tin for silence.*

Shh!

It goes a bit quieter.

NATE *urgently goes to join her at the radio.*

TUSH. We have a responsibility to be happy. We're the survivors. If we're miserable, then Hitler won.

SOLLY. Hitler did win.

RITA. Did you get the liquorice, Tush?

SOLLY *scrabbles in his pocket and pulls out a crumpled paper bag. He hands it to RITA with great care.*

Thanks.

SOLLY. It's nothing.

RITA *takes out a piece and sucks.*

TUSH. You know what Rousseau said?

MAY *groans*. VINCE *laughs*.

According to Rousseau, and I paraphrase, the Jews in the diaspora have no chance of revealing their truth to mankind. Forget it. And it's only when we rule ourselves, have our own government, that we can speak out safely and then the world will listen at last to what we have to say, and learn what we can teach.

SOLLY. What have we got to teach the world? How easy it is to climb on a train and go up in smoke?

TUSH. We have learned from our suffering . . .

SOLLY *snorts*.

RITA. What have we learned, Tush?

TUSH. How to survive. How to be enterprising. How to break through the restrictions of the old, set ways.

SOLLY. And who else is breaking through the old, set ways for the common good? Oh, I remember. A certain Comrade Joe Stalin.

VINCE. Don't believe everything his enemies claim.

TUSH. We Jews bring something unique: the originality of the outsider. At present we have no status in the world, worse than no status. But we have the spirit to stand up for ourselves at last, to stand up too for all the oppressed minorities, and raise the torch of equality and justice for all.

SOLLY *snorts with derision*.

MAY. Never mind People and Nations. What about the fire a *person* feels? The need to shine. What about the vital flame? Someone tell me, how to keep that alight?

VINCE. And why must it dim as the years pass?

MAY. Yes. Exactly.

NATE *and* BEIL *are getting worked up by the radio, clearly following the 2.30 very closely.*

NATE. Come on, Yankee Relish!

TUSH. Maybe I'll actually go to Palestine when I'm demobbed. And pick up that shovel with my own bare hands.

SOLLY. You wouldn't know one end of a shovel from the other, little prince.

RITA. You will, Tush. I believe you will.

SOLLY. Who cares?

RITA. Some people do care, you know. And we don't need reminding all the time that you don't.

SOLLY retreats like a wounded animal with a handful of chocolate.

NATE. Damn it!

BEIL. Ha ha!!

NATE tears up two betting slips.

NATE. Bloody Yankee Relish! Bloody Fair Week!

BEIL. Did I tell you Wicklow Star or did I tell you Wicklow Star?

NATE. What do you bloody well know?

BEIL. Enough.

NATE. Enough.

The doorbell rings.

BEIL bustles out to answer it.

I'm never putting my money on another quadraped for as long as I live.

MAY. And what will poor old Gyppo do without you?

NATE. Ah, I almost forgot about Gyppo. My messiah and saviour.

MAY. Do you never give up?

Voices from the hallway.

FREDDY (*offstage*). Yer alright, Auntie B?

BEIL (*offstage*). Fine fettle, Freddy. Fine fettle, as they say.

FREDDY (*offstage*). Is Rita around?

    BEIL *pokes her head round the door.*

BEIL. Rita? Freddy's here for you.

RITA. Invite him in.

BEIL. You know what he's like about 'foreigners'.

    Various murmurs of jovial protest and 'Come on in, Freddy!'
    from TUSH *and* VINCE.

    Go on out to the hall. Go to him. Go on.

    RITA *sighs and exits.*

    (*To all present.*) He's brought a little something to cheer
her up.

MAY. Ah, bless his little cotton socks.

BEIL. And bless hers too.

NATE. Why do you even let the little sweetheart slog away
like that?

    RITA *enters carrying a children's spinning top and some-*
    thing else.

MAY. Invite him in.

RITA. He had to get off to his sister's to listen to the race.

NATE. I hope he told you not to work too hard.

MAY. A spinning top?

RITA. And that's not all!

    She holds up a tin mug, with a picture of the Statue of
    Liberty stuck on it, crammed with coloured crayons.

    I swear that he thinks I'm still at junior school.

NATE. Give me a set of crayons any day and I'll be happily occupied for a week.

VINCE. How old are you, Dr Nate?

NATE. Twenty-one! And I'll take on any man who says otherwise.

RITA. Look!

Everyone laughs.

RITA *spins the top. Everyone stares, mesmerised.*

Silence.

MAY. Is the tea coming?

BEIL. I'm getting. I'm getting.

BEIL *bustles out.*

VINCE *is looking out of the window.*

VINCE. It's starting to rain again.

Everyone groans.

NATE. Heavy going today, folks.

He turns up the wireless to hear the preamble to the big race.

DEBBIE *walks in with a swaddled bundle of baby clutched to her breast and shoulder and nearly treads on the top. She kicks it under a chair.*

DEBBIE. Sh. Shush, please. Bobby's just beginning to settle.

NATE *reluctantly turns down the knob a tiny tad.*

(*In her little Bobby voice.*) 'Oooh. Could you just lower it a bit more? That's still so loud, Great Uncle Nate,' asks Bobby.

NATE *mutters and does not turn the knob.*

'Oooh. Thank you, Great Uncle Nate. Thank you so much for understanding how much I need peace and quiet to recover from my chesty cough that I caught in this big draughty house.'

NATE *turns down the volume.*

NATE. Do you want me to take a look at him for you?

DEBBIE. That's very kind, but there's no need to go to any trouble.

NATE. No trouble. I'll get my stethoscope. And then we can get him to bed.

DEBBIE. Nah, he just needs a little cuddle from his mummy. He's not been himself. He's a sensitive little chap. And Bobby's more sensitive than most. I swear that when I look into his wise little eyes, that child seems to know more than the rest of us put together.

SOLLY. If that child were mine, I'd rip off his head and throw him in the Mersey. That'd toughen him up.

DEBBIE *clutches* BOBBY *to her.*

DEBBIE. Are you some kind of maniac?

TUSH. Solly, did you eat all the chocolate already?

SOLLY. There was hardly any left anyhow.

SOLLY *retreats, sneaks out his bottle of aftershave and gives himself a quick dab.*

DEBBIE *sniffs with distaste, coughs, hugs* BOBBY *even tighter.*

NATE*'s fingers slide towards the volume knob on the wireless.*

But DEBBIE *sees and gives him a warning look.*

NATE. Has it stopped raining yet?

VINCE. Nope.

MAY. Whether the weather is cold . . .

RITA. Or whether the weather is hot . . .

RITA *shakes her pencil tin like a maraca.* NATE *joins in shaking the JNF tin again.*

MAY. We'll weather the weather . . .

RITA. Whatever the weather . . .

MAY *and* RITA. Whether we like it or not!

MAY. But when we get to New York we won't even notice if it rains because we'll be so happy to be there again.

Somewhere in the distance a phone is ringing.

VINCE. I'll bet that during the war you felt the same about being happy in peacetime. Didn't you long to let the lights shine at night, never to hear an air-raid siren again? And now the war is over, do you even notice these things?

BEIL *wheels in a trolley with a couple of steaming teapots, cups and saucers, etc.*

BEIL. Commandeer, there was a phone call for you from the base. The lady said to call your wife. It's an emergency.

MAY *is all ears.*

VINCE. Ah.

BEIL. You can use the telephone in the study.

VINCE. Thank you, Beil. Excuse me.

VINCE *exits with urgency.*

BEIL. What a devoted husband.

MAY. What do you know about it? Nothing!

BEIL *pours a cup of tea.*

BEIL. Would you like a splash more milk, May?

MAY. Stop fussing.

MAY *snatches the cup.*

DEBBIE. Manners.

MAY. You can talk.

DEBBIE. Please don't raise your voice like that around the baby. What on earth is wrong with you, May?

NATE. What's right with her!

MAY. Oh, grow up, you silly old man. Pay the rent and leave us alone.

NATE *reaches again towards the volume knob on the wireless.*

DEBBIE *coughs loudly.*

DEBBIE. I really do not understand you, if you don't mind me saying so, May. To look at, you could almost be Ava Gardner. Why do you have to go and spoil it all by being so crabby most of the time?

MAY. Unbelievable!

MAY *holds her cup out to* BEIL *who pours some milk into it.*

NATE *surreptitiously drops some schnapps into his tea.*

RITA. What's happened to Vince?

MAY. He's trying to telephone his wife.

TUSH. Good luck to him. I couldn't believe how long the operator kept me waiting last weekend. Mind you, look on the bright side – he might never get through.

SOLLY. Or his wife won't answer cos she's a stiff.

TUSH *pulls something out of his pocket. It is a piece of folded paper.*

TUSH. Hey, Solly, look what I found.

SOLLY *looks suspiciously at the paper.*

Take it, gun-bunny.

SOLLY *takes it and unfolds the paper. Inside is a piece of chocolate.*

So there is some chocolate to be found after all. Let's make up. Here.

SOLLY. A peace offering? Did we fall out?

TUSH. Admit it, you do stir things up, Sol . . . Hey, forget it. Have the chocolate, my friend.

SOLLY *eats a piece.*

SOLLY. Thank you, kind Romeo.

TUSH. What's Romeo got to with anything!

SOLLY. Blah-blah-blah.

TUSH. Look, I'm trying not to get mad but I just hate the way you dig at me whenever we come here . . .

SOLLY. It's the words. They pop out of my mouth. They got a life of their own. You understand how it is with me, right? At least I'm honest.

TUSH. I can't help liking you, Sol. God knows why. But I swear, I don't know anyone else who makes me want to punch his lights out like you do.

SOLLY. I'll slit your throat before you can raise your fist.

SOLLY *pulls something out of his pocket and suddenly aims at* TUSH. *It could be a gun, or a knife . . . but it's a flask.*

Bourbon?

TUSH *receives the flask willingly and swigs.*

ARNOLD *enters.*

DEBBIE *has sidled up to the radio where she is rocking to and fro with baby* BOBBY. *She gestures to* ARNOLD *to join her. He does so and she whispers in his ear.*

TUSH *passes the flask back to* SOLLY *who swigs.*

TUSH. I really think that I will head off to Palestine when we're done here. I'm gonna write my folks today.

SOLLY. The best thing to do with dreams, Romeo, is to obliterate them, before they obliterate the shit out of you.

DEBBIE *gasps.*

DEBBIE. Do something about this lunatic, Arnold!

ARNOLD. Will you please keep your foul mouth shut in my house, sir? Or I'll make you wash it out with soap.

Everyone stares at SOLLY.

He shrinks into himself and leaves the room.

ARNOLD *switches off the wireless. He coughs slightly.*

DEBBIE *starts to hum a lullaby to* BOBBY.

RITA. Isn't the race about to start?

Silence.

Everyone looks at DEBBIE *as she rocks her* BOBBY *by the wireless.*

ARNOLD. It's just a little bit difficult today . . .

RITA. But we always listened to the Grand National with Daddy and everyone . . .

MAY. And have our annual flutter . . .

RITA. And we all really missed it when it stopped during the war. And now it's on again and . . . Oh Arnold!

MAY. Arnold?

DEBBIE *stands right beside the wireless, rocking and rocking* BOBBY.

ARNOLD. The bets still count.

NATE. Oh, yes indeed, the bets still count.

DEBBIE. And if you don't mind my saying so, you can easily get tomorrow's paper, or even this evening's, for the report of the race. And all the results.

NATE. Nothing could be easier.

DEBBIE (*in her little Bobby voice*). 'Oh, thank you everybody for thinking of me when I'm feeling so poorly. I so need my peace and quiet.'

BEIL. Don't we all.

BEIL *exits, with teapots.*

DEBBIE *hums her soothing lullaby and rocks* BOBBY.

Everyone else glances by turn at the wireless and their watches or the clock.

NATE. Maybe I'll just nip down the road to a more 'amenable' location.

TUSH. Better make a move too.

DEBBIE. Ah, Bobby, isn't everyone kind?

DEBBIE *sweeps out of the room.*

RITA. Can't we switch on the wireless just a little bit?

ARNOLD. Better not.

RITA. But it's my wireless.

ARNOLD. And we all have to live here. And there's the baby to consider.

NATE. Don't worry, little Rita, you'll always be the baby of the house to me.

RITA *groans and slumps in a chair, rattling her tin of pencils with irritation.*

MAY (*imitating* DEBBIE's 'Bobby voice'). 'Off we go, everybody! Best gerra move on if we want to hear the horsies fall and break their necksies in the nasty rain.'

ARNOLD. I might just accompany you 'down the road', Nate.

NATE. Looks like you could do with a little light relief, my son.

ARNOLD *coughs to clear his wheezing. Then he takes a packet of cigarettes and a lighter out of his pocket.*

D'you want me to prescribe a little something for that wheezing?

ARNOLD. Any tips for the Spring Cup at 3.50?

ARNOLD *lights up.*

RITA. Oh Arnold!

ARNOLD. Oh Rita!

NATE. Let's see what my special friend down at the turf accountant's can recommend, ma boy. Don't worry, we'll see you right.

MAY. Oh Nate.

NATE. What? Am I the one who has thrown us out on our ears?

ARNOLD. I'll get my coat.

MAY (*to* ARNOLD). Just don't say that we didn't warn you.

ARNOLD. What do you mean? Getting married was the best thing I ever did.

ARNOLD *wheezes some more. And puffs.*

NATE. All the same, a man learns to embrace his lot, my dear boy. Even a lonely old alter Kaker like me learns to live with himself.

RITA. You have us, Uncle Nate.

NATE. Thank God something remains of your poor, dear mother. Not that it matters any more. What does it matter? Ta-ta, folks.

NATE *exits.*

MAY. Oh Arnold, please . . .

ARNOLD. What's wrong with following a couple of races, May?

She touches his arm.

MAY. Arnold?

ARNOLD. Honestly.

ARNOLD *exits*.

MAY. Who fancies seeing if there might be a sultana slice at the Lyons' Corner House?

TUSH. Let me treat you both.

RITA. I swear that I can't even stand up.

MAY. Looks like it's just you and me, Romeo.

RITA. Go on, Tush.

MAY. Come on. I'll try not to eat you.

TUSH. Catch you tomorrow, Rita?

RITA. I'll probably be asleep in bed all day.

MAY *takes* TUSH *by the hand and drags him out of the door.*

RITA *stretches her legs, considers the wireless, slowly reaches out to switch it on . . .*

SOLLY *enters*.

SOLLY. Where have they all gone?

RITA. Anywhere but here.

Silence.

Please don't feel obliged to keep me company.

SOLLY. There's nowhere else on earth I'd rather be.

RITA. I know where I'd rather be.

SOLLY. You're lucky.

RITA. Am I?

SOLLY. You have the thought of New York to make your heart beat faster.

RITA. It's more than just a thought to me.

Silence.

SOLLY. I used to feel that way about waving the red flag in Moscow. That's become the second biggest joke in the world.

RITA. And what's the biggest joke?

SOLLY. Work makes you free.

RITA. Why do you say it like that? So sour?

SOLLY. '*Arbeit Macht Frei*.' On the entrance to Auschwitz. And now Tush and his Zionists make it their own.

RITA. What have you seen, Solly?

SOLLY *stares at her.*

I saw the newsreel. All the piles of bodies. It gave me nightmares.

SOLLY *continues to stare.*

Solly, please. What have you seen?

SOLLY. I see . . . I see . . . such simple . . . such pure . . . goodness . . . in you . . . my beautiful Rita . . . you are the light . . . You . . .

RITA. But . . .

SOLLY. . . . innocent, sweet girl . . . This is the place I want to be. Here. With you . . . You'll make me clean . . . You're pure . . . You see where the truth lies . . . You're the only person in the world who can possibly understand me . . . I love you . . . I love you without end . . . I love without beginning . . . I love . . .

RITA. Please stop it!

SOLLY. I won't live without you.

RITA. D'you think the race is over now? Shall we try to find out the result?

She turns to the wireless and desperately starts fiddling with the knobs.

SOLLY. Can you hear me? . . . Don't you understand what I'm saying? I know I don't always talk fancy like Tush . . . Are these words wrong? . . . What else am I meant to say . . . ?

RITA. I seem to have lost the place . . .

RITA *is whizzing through the frequencies . . . music . . . voices . . . all crowd upon each other.*

SOLLY. Okay . . . I get the message . . . But don't think that I can watch any other guy . . . whose love . . . Damn him . . . Damn him! . . . His love is dirt . . . He is nothing . . . If only you could see it . . . No one else deserves to come anywhere near you . . . before you realise what I can give you . . . Because I will not let him do that . . . I swear . . . I swear . . .

RITA *turns up the volume. The wireless is all out of tuning, hisses and squeaks.*

Very abruptly, brutally, SOLLY *switches it off.*

DEBBIE *enters.*

DEBBIE. Oh gosh! I didn't think that there was anyone left in here.

SOLLY. Who cares what you think!

SOLLY *exits.*

RITA *grabs hold of* DEBBIE *for support.*

DEBBIE. You look like the world has wiped the floor with you, poor sausage.

RITA. I need to lie down.

RITA *heads very wearily for the door.*

DEBBIE. Oh, just a mo, Rita. Bobby has a big favour to ask of his bestest auntie.

RITA. What is it?

DEBBIE. It's just that his room is so cold and smells of damp and your room is dry and warm . . .

VINCE *enters*.

VINCE. I'm sorry it took so long to get through . . . Where is everybody?

GERTIE *enters, followed by* MORDY.

GERTIE. Debbie, Peter O'Donnell is at the door for you. He says that he's got a gift for the new baby in his new car.

DEBBIE. He's brought the car here? Where?

GERTIE. It's not, I'm afraid, very difficult to spot out there.

DEBBIE *dashes out of the room*.

MORDY. Where is everybody?

RITA. They went.

VINCE. But they were all here . . .

MORDY. Why didn't May meet us for lunch at the Karps' as we arranged?

VINCE. Which horse won the race?

RITA. How should I know?

RITA *slumps back into the big armchair*.

GERTIE. Where's Arnold, Rita?

RITA. He went off with Nate.

GERTIE. We really have got to do something about him. After shul, they were all talking about what he lost at the game last week. Fifteen pounds! Where did he get fifteen pounds from? Someone's got to have a proper word with him . . . And why's it so hot in this house? How many fires are going? What do people think, that coal grows on trees . . .

MORDY. Well, technically, Gertie, coal is the remains of trees . . .

GERTIE. Oh Mordy.

MORDY. Do you dispute the fact?

GERTIE *can't help but smile a little.*

GERTIE. Where's Auntie B?

GERTIE *goes out.*

VINCE. Well, thank God the panic's over and my wife is settled at last. And the rain seems to have stopped. Want to take a quiet stroll with me, Mordy, about town?

MORDY. Oh well, I don't know. Better hadn't. Seeing as May seems to have evaporated, I'll take the opportunity to go home and catch up with my shiur before Havdallah at the Dorfmans'. If you see May, Rita, please tell her that she can meet me there.

RITA. Okee-dokee.

VINCE. I'll just head off into town then. Check out the Lyons'.

MORDY. Fare thee well, Rita.

VINCE. Bye.

As MORDY *and* VINCE *depart,* DEBBIE *pops in. She is wearing her coat and hat, putting on her gloves.*

DEBBIE. Oh Rita, if Bobby cries, be a love and give him a cuddle for us? I won't be more than half an hour. But I just can't resist taking a little spin. It'd be rude to refuse such a big nob on the council, wouldn't it? And you never know when he might come in handy. See you later.

DEBBIE *disappears.*

RITA *is all alone. She begins to sing Cole Porter's 'I Happen to Like New York' to herself.*

ACT THREE

Monday, 4th August, 1947.

Around midnight.

The drawing room/dining room is now facing the other way. The dining table and chairs are scattered with newspapers and books and baby paraphernalia.

MAY, *looking weary, wearing no shoes, is sitting at the piano in the drawing room beyond the half-closed partition.*

MAY *taps the metronome.*

It ticks.

Sounds of voices in the hallway. Urgent. FREDDY, *'It's Chaos', 'Loada thugs', 'Just hold tight', 'Yer alright'.* GERTIE*'s voice too, 'Hold tight?', 'Help out'. And both, 'Can't believe it.' Then goodbyes.*

GERTIE *comes in, carrying a pile of blankets and sheets.*

BEIL *follows her with some pillows and pillowcases.*

GERTIE. Sounds like it's pandemonium out there.

BEIL. How far away did Freddy say they are now?

GERTIE. Still round Brownlow Hill.

BEIL. Are they coming this way?

GERTIE. Who knows.

BEIL. God protect us all! What's happening, May? May!

    MAY *quietly dabs at her hand which has a slight cut.*

MAY. I've told you. There are hundreds of them . . . They've got bricks and bats and bottles. And there's a lot of shouting . . . And lots of windows broken . . .

BEIL. It's Kishinev all over again!

MAY. The glass is everywhere . . . The front room is ruined.

GERTIE. Thank God you got to us . . .

> MAY *tinkers at the piano, Gershwin's 'Summertime'. She hums softly.*

BEIL. It can't happen here. Hah!

> *They start tidying the table and chairs to make room for their piles of bedding.*

GERTIE. Let's hope it's just a localised outburst.

BEIL. 'Localised outburst'! No one ever learns. No one ever listens to me. I know. I've seen good people turn into animals. Rip a poor little boy to pieces. And now it's happening here. You heard Freddy. Listen to May! May . . . !

> MAY *continues playing.*

GERTIE. Leave her alone. She's been through enough.

BEIL. Cossacks with Scouse accents.

> BEIL *harrumphs.*

GERTIE. Did Moseley come to power here? No.

BEIL. Not yet.

GERTIE. Don't be so ridiculous.

MAY (*singing*). . . . so hush little baby
      Don't you cry!

GERTIE. We have to work out where we can put people. May and Mordy will just have to go in Rita's room that Bobby's using. And we must make space in case anyone who lives round there needs somewhere safe for the night. They can have my room. I don't mind sleeping down here. And Vince will be too exhausted after helping out on the front line to drive back to Burtonwood . . .

MAY *stops playing*.

And what about Tush?

MAY. He can sleep in Rita's bed.

GERTIE. Behave yourself!

MAY *starts to play again, some Rachmaninov.*

Oh, if only we had more beds for all the people who need one . . .

BEIL. Don't make me go back into my old room with boards for a window. Please, Gertie.

GERTIE. Don't be silly, B. It's too dusty in there for anyone. And dark. But one of the guys might not mind if they're shattered.

BEIL. Don't put me in the home for aged Jews before it's even built.

GERTIE. No one's putting you anywhere, Auntie.

DEBBIE *enters*.

DEBBIE. Gosh, that's a lot of laundry.

GERTIE. We're preparing for the onslaught.

DEBBIE. How many are you expecting?

GERTIE. As many as need.

DEBBIE. With all the German measles going around?

GERTIE. What are you talking about?

DEBBIE. It's an epidemic. Haven't you noticed how many children and teachers have been missing school?

GERTIE. Oh, it doesn't do any harm to catch it and get it out of the way . . .

DEBBIE. That's all very well for you to say.

BEIL *gathers together a pile of bed linen*.

BEIL. I'm off to make up the bed for May and Mordy now.

GERTIE. Oh yes. Debbie, we're just putting them into Rita's old room. Just for the night.

DEBBIE. Whoa! Hold your horses this instant.

BEIL *hangs onto the sheets and looks to* GERTIE.

GERTIE *nods.* BEIL *turns to go.*

You heard me, bubba! Stop right there!

BEIL *offers the sheets to* DEBBIE.

BEIL. You make up the bed for May and Mordy then.

DEBBIE *does not take the sheets.*

DEBBIE. They can go in the shrapnel room.

MAY *keeps playing the piano. She moves onto practice scales, not a falter.*

BEIL *holds out the sheets again to* DEBBIE.

BEIL. So here!

DEBBIE. Oh, no no. Don't you think I've got enough to do every day without having to pick up the pieces after your feeble excuse for housekeeping? I'm shattered enough as it is.

BEIL. What did I tell you about fussing over the baby? You make the rod for your own back. Leave him in his cot in his own room, close the door and let him cry until he drops off. (*She spits three times.*) Easy.

DEBBIE. Keep your spit to yourself, you disgusting old witch.

BEIL *throws the sheets on the floor at* DEBBIE's *feet and storms out.*

(*Shouting after* BEIL.) The sooner they build that retirement home at Stapeley, the better!

GERTIE. I can't believe what I'm hearing.

DEBBIE. I have no idea how you have the patience. You really are some kind of saint, Gertie. The way you work all day teaching those mobs of children and then putting up with your senile old auntie when you come home . . .

GERTIE. Beil has lived here even longer than we have. Show her some respect.

DEBBIE. Respect, if you don't mind me saying, is a two-way street.

MAY *stops playing, glares at* DEBBIE *and walks out of the room.*

GERTIE. I don't have the energy for this.

GERTIE *picks up the sheets and heads for the door.*

DEBBIE. Oh, be a love and make up the bed for May and Mordy in the shrapnel room.

GERTIE. But there's no one in Rita's old room. Aren't you still putting Bobby to sleep in your bed?

DEBBIE. But it's still Bobby's room and Arnold uses it most nights.

GERTIE. This is an emergency, Debbie.

DEBBIE. Oh Gertie, it's so important for children to keep in with their routine.

GERTIE. What routine? It seems to change by the minute.

DEBBIE. With all due respect, being a mother is a round-the-clock job. You can't just sign off at the end of the day when you're dealing with your own child.

GERTIE. And you can't just retire your beloved auntie to the knacker's yard when she gets beyond a certain age.

DEBBIE. You'll thank me for it when the spoon-feeding starts.

GERTIE. I'll thank you to keep out of our family business.

DEBBIE. Oh my. We really are getting ourselves in a right pickle, aren't we?

GERTIE. This is all very wearing.

DEBBIE. So we'd better come to some sort of understanding.

GERTIE. Oh dear, had we?

DEBBIE. You get on with being a teacher and becoming head-mistress like you really deserve . . .

GERTIE. That is hardly on the cards . . .

DEBBIE. . . . And I will keep an eye on things around the house and make sure that Dr Weinberg actually pays his rent until he can move out somewhere more suitable . . . Oh yes, the new Jewish old-age home is going to have a hospital attached, you know . . .

GERTIE. But Nate will never give up his lovely room with the William Morris wallpaper . . .

DEBBIE. Oh Gertie, please, stop fighting me all the time, I'm trying to knock this place into shape . . . And if only you people will let me get on with it and stop making such a silly fuss about every little thing I try to change . . . If you don't mind me saying, you have let this beautiful house go to seed . . . It needs a whole new fresh start . . . Someone who really knows what they're doing . . .

MORDY *enters. He is damp and weary but excited. It's clearly raining outside.*

GERTIE. Where on earth have you been for so long?

MORDY. Where's May?

GERTIE. She's gone to rest upstairs somewhere.

MORDY. Well, I did try to get back to the house to see what damage has been done but there's no way to get through safely. It's chaos. I had to give your dad a hand, Debbie . . .

DEBBIE. Is the business alright? Is he alright?

MORDY. It'll take more than a mob to see off Joe Pollack. I helped him schlep the chickens and saveloys he'd managed to save from the shop. Typical Joe, he was that determined to go back into the fray for the beef joints he'd just got in. It took two Rosenblatts, plus Meyer Max and me to stop him from putting himself in harm's way. And then Ena Lebetkin did nothing to help calm him down by claiming that the abattoir is refusing to allow kosher slaughter in protest at what those terrorists of ours have done.

DEBBIE. Oh no!

MORDY. Joe was up in arms!

DEBBIE. I'm up in arms!

MORDY. Everyone's up in arms. Or lost. The Levy sisters were still in their slippers wandering the streets. What a relief that we managed to get them to the Bennetts'. Then Rhona began on about the time she was caught short in Williamson Square when the air-raid warning sounded. They're probably still at it, telling stories. But I thought I'd better brave the mobs and make it to you. I was told more than once to go to Palestine where I belonged. I resisted the impulse to inform them that the furthest abroad I intend to go in the near future is Salford for my cousin Betty's birthday tea.

GERTIE. Here, give me your jacket.

MORDY. Is May alright?

GERTIE. More or less.

MORDY *lets* GERTIE *remove his jacket.*

MORDY. The school's alright, thank God. No one seems to have thought of coming up this way yet. Not that thinking seems to be very much in evidence all round.

GERTIE. May said the house is in a terrible state.

MORDY. What can you do? Oh well. A few broken windows are easily fixed.

GERTIE. Shall I make you some sweet tea?

MORDY. Bless you. Bless you, Gertie. You are the only one in the world who knows how to make me feel better.

GERTIE. Mordy, don't be so silly, what would May say if she heard you go on like that?

MORDY. Oh, you know what I mean.

GERTIE. Honey or sugar?

MORDY. I have a choice?

GERTIE. I have a secret stash.

MORDY. Honey, please. You are a saint.

GERTIE. So I'm often told.

DEBBIE. But you are!

NATE hovers in the doorway to the drawing room, swaying slightly. He looks blankly round the room.

MORDY (*whispering*). Oh heavens, the good doctor is lurching our way. He's soused as a herring, Gert.

GERTIE. But he's been off the bottle for years . . .

NATE opens his arms to the empty drawing room.

NATE. Will somebody please explain to me what this world is coming to?

MORDY (*giggles*). I'm diving for cover.

MORDY falls to his knees and crawls under the table. He reaches up a hand to GERTIE.

Come on, come on, Gert, before he spots you too.

GERTIE. Stop being so puerile. Honestly. What's got into you, Mordechai Fischer?

NATE (*declaiming some more*). Did I hang a single Britisher soldier with these bare hands? Am I my brothers' keeper?

GERTIE *grabs* DEBBIE *by the hand and shushes. They creep out.*

NATE *pushes back the partition roughly and has to grapple with it to get it open.*

Hah! As I suspected. No one here! Unless the little buggers are hiding.

He veers towards the table as if about to look under it and then veers away again.

Bloody terrorists. Causing all this damn trouble. I ask you – was it me who hanged those two Britisher sergeants? Am I to blame? Bleeding Jews! Does not a Jew bleed like all the other bleeders? Just because some lunatic Israelites halfway across the world get out the noose for a couple of our boys, why do Yiddishe windows over here have to get smashed? Bloody Jews!

He holds up his hands.

Clean hands, I say. Clean as a virgin's honour. Innocent until proven guilty. British justice. The finest justice in the world. Splendid country. Upright, honest folk. I am proud to be British.

He pulls a ten-shilling note out of his pocket.

And now they tell me, 'Keep your dirty lucre after what your lot have done to our lads in Pally-stine! None of your bets here after what YOUR LOT done.'

He waves the ten-shilling note.

Dirty filthy lucre! Hah! Where's it from? Don't ask. Do I get the girls up the duff? Not me. I just get them out of their spot of bother. Three months gone, all gone. Clean as a whistle. It wasn't me, guv, honest. Ten shillings on Ballyhoo is all I ask. Everyday we rub shoulders, don't we, Messrs Byrne, Huff and Coyle and the like. And is there ever a protest when I lay down my ill-gotten gains?

He kisses the ten shillings.

All mine, for killing the unborn up a bloody back alley! Hippocratic oath be damned! Dr Weinberg be bloody damned! But does anyone care? Not a squeak. What matter the baby I washed down the plughole? But a full-grown sergeant or two what I never went near? Dear me, no. Do our dirty work for us on the hush. But we'll forget all that when your distant brothers get out of hand. My lot? I ask you.

NATE *tears up the ten shillings.*

This is my lot!!! Sod the lot of you!

He collapses into a chair.

RITA *and* TUSH *enter.*

He is wearing civvies, smart clothes that are less dishevelled than they might be after being in the midst of a riot.

TUSH. Can you get over that sign in the grocer's window?

RITA. I still can't believe it.

TUSH. Bold and clear – 'We are not Jews.' So you don't need to break our windows.

RITA. I never thought people round here would be so quick to wipe their hands of us.

TUSH. This is how it always goes.

RITA. And if Hitler had invaded. Well, it's obvious now . . . They've all proved Auntie Beil right. God help us all.

NATE. And if you lot set up this blasted Homeland, watch out for even more trouble. Bloody wars from beginning to end.

TUSH. Don't blame us for their hatred.

NATE. By the waters of Babylon I sat down and wept!

RITA. Are you alright, Uncle Nate?

NATE. Not a spot on me, little munchkin.

TUSH. Hadn't you better go to bed?

NATE. Hadn't you better get your skates on to the Holy Land forthwith, young man? Spot of bother over there. And none of us are safe from it. Bloody troublemakers.

RITA. The British occupiers are the troublemakers. They should get out and let us get on with making our own state.

TUSH. The Brits have only themselves to blame.

RITA. We have no choice but to resist them and fight back.

NATE. Oooh la la! Hark at the Yiddishe Joan of Arc.

> VINCE *enters. He is dishevelled and over-tired.*

VINCE. Has anyone seen Freddy?

> RITA *and* TUSH *shake their heads.*

> SOLLY *sidles in and hovers at the edge of the room, dabbing on twice as much aftershave as usual.*

RITA. What are you doing here?

SOLLY (*pointing at* TUSH). He's here. Why not me?

TUSH (*to* VINCE). What's going on?

VINCE. There were a bunch of them . . . Freddy and his mates . . . Said they weren't letting these hooligans attack innocent neighbours . . . And we joined them . . . went down to the bottom of Brownlow Hill where a huge crowd was throwing rocks . . . And together we put up a barricade . . . stood in the path of the mob . . . And Freddy ordered them to keep out . . .

> MORDY *emerges from under the table.*

MORDY. That's the spirit!

TUSH *and* RITA. Mordy?!

TUSH. What the . . . ?

NATE. Where did he come from?

MORDY. Pull together, boys and girls! Beat the Blitz!

RITA. But all the damage that's been done . . .

TUSH. We must organise a fundraiser . . . maybe a concert . . . at Zion House . . .

RITA. Somewhere bigger. What about the Max Morris Hall? Or the Rialto?

TUSH. And we can ask May to play . . .

RITA. She hasn't played in public for years.

TUSH. It's about time she did something worthwhile with her talent instead of complaining that no one understands her.

MORDY. And she plays so beautifully . . . She's always playing and singing at home . . . for hours and hours . . . But only ever to herself.

RITA. She absolutely must perform to an audience again. And this is such an important cause. I'll persuade her.

TUSH. And we can use half the proceeds to help people who've suffered damage here, and half can go to Jewish defence in Palestine . . . Or maybe a quarter for the ones here and three quarters for Palestine . . .

NATE. Never mind bloody Palestine, give it all to me!

VINCE *and* MORDY *both spot* MAY*'s hat, gloves and shoes not far from the piano.*

NATE *picks up the metronome and starts to fiddle with the tempo mechanism.*

VINCE. Is May upstairs?

VINCE *sits at the piano thoughtfully.*

MORDY. Better not disturb her.

VINCE *plays some of the tune of 'I Happen to Like New York'.*

VINCE. Looks like my unit might be transferred.

TUSH. Back home?

VINCE. Yeah.

TUSH. Your wife must be busting with joy.

VINCE. I haven't told anyone yet.

VINCE *repeats the tune he's just played. This section must be all he knows.*

But, who knows, I might take your lead, Tush, and resign.

RITA. And we'll be off to New York before too long. How quiet it'll be when everyone's gone.

VINCE *plays loudly.*

NATE *pushes the pendulum needle beyond its limits, manages to pull it off the metronome.*

NATE. How do you put this blasted thing back on?

RITA. Oh Uncle Nate! Mummy's metronome.

NATE. Well, help me glue it back together or something.

RITA. Glue won't help. Oh Uncle Nate.

MORDY. Dearie dearie dearie me, Nathan Weinberg. F-double-minus for vandalism.

NATE. What's the matter with you all? (*He waves the broken parts of the metronome.*) Does this look like the end of the world? Why the great drama? It probably isn't even broken. We're only kidding ourselves that it is. None of this ever happened.

Silence.

And this is probably still my house. The one I grew up in. The one that Daddy's daddy built. The one Cyril and Esty took on when they got married. And promised to cherish. God bless them. Our beautiful house on Hope Street. And what kind of bloody deluded name for a road is that? And while I'm on the subject of the absurd, tell me, does anybody else find it more than a little farcical that our Debbie Lasky, nee Pollack, is taking rather a lot of rides in the automobile department – and the rest – with our ubiquitous councillor, O'Donnell? Would anyone care to comment?

Very awkward silence.

Well, I don't know about you, but I'm going to find some desperately needed glue.

NATE *exits, wielding the broken pieces of the metronome.*

RITA. Why is everything falling apart?

MORDY. Don't get too alarmed now, Rita.

RITA. But that was Mummy's metronome that Daddy gave to her when I was born. And the riots. What will become of us? We have no choice now but to leave the country. Even if we didn't want to. We're being driven out.

MORDY. I would hardly go that far.

TUSH. I would go a lot further.

MORDY. Nothing like this has happened here in living memory.

TUSH. It was always gonna happen sooner or later.

MORDY. Well, haven't I warned you? There's a huge price to pay once we start declaring ourselves to be a separate nation with allegiances elsewhere.

VINCE. And what choice do we have but to pay that price?

MORDY. There's always a choice about whether you go blustering and bombarding. Some of us prefer to proceed with care and caution . . . and decency.

SOLLY. Trample or be trampled.

TUSH. How much more do you want to go wrong before you admit it? . . . We need our own state . . . We need self determination . . . We need . . .

VINCE. Enough damn talking! Words, words, words! What use are they? I just found a little girl of not more than seven years old, about the same age as my daughter Sarah. And this child was bleeding all over her dress. She'd cut her hand on broken glass. She'd lost her daddy. 'He's going to my auntie's,' she kept saying. And I said three words. 'We'll find him.' And I did.

MAY *enters quietly, wearily. She heads towards* VINCE, *seeing only him. Then she notices* MORDY *and the rest and stops short.*

You thought you were safe from attack here? Now look. You think it can't happen in New York either? It can happen anywhere. That could have been one of my daughters bleeding in the street . . . How can I let that happen? Even if we must become fighting machines, even if we must travel across oceans . . . The world must be made safe for our children.

MORDY. And the sergeants that those Zionist extremists left hanging from a eucalyptus tree? Were they fathers? And husbands? What about their daughters or sons? Don't they count too?

SOLLY. 'Blood on the leaves and blood on the root.'

MORDY. Blood on our hands. What kind of safe haven can be forged out of murder? When will it ever end?

SOLLY. Never-ending never-ending never-ending . . .

VINCE. There will be an end if we face the trouble head on . . .

MAY (*singing*). There may be trouble ahead . . .

VINCE. When isn't there trouble?

MAY *continues singing the next lines of Irving Berlin's 'Let's Face the Music and Dance'.*

Silence.

(*Speaking directly to* MAY.) Let's face the music and dance.

TUSH *continues singing the song, grabs hold of* RITA *and starts to dance with her.*

SOLLY *surges at the dancing couple and taps* TUSH *unceremoniously on the shoulder.*

TUSH. What are you doing?

SOLLY. It's my turn.

VINCE. It's getting late.

TUSH gives RITA one more twirl.

All the activity seems to exhaust MORDY. He drops into a chair and his eyelids grow heavy.

TUSH (*singing*). Let's face the music and dance . . .

VINCE. Let's call it a day.

SOLLY. Sure thing, sir. (*To* TUSH.) I'm watching you.

VINCE. Lighten up, soldier. Time to hit the deck.

VINCE exits with SOLLY, as MAY and TUSH resume their singing.

TUSH continues to dance with RITA, more slowly now, less display and more intimacy. Soon, RITA stops dancing.

MAY. Shouldn't you be hitting the deck too, Tush?

TUSH. Just make the decision, Rita. You could pack your bag tonight. And tomorrow we set off for agricultural training.

MAY. Goodnight, Theodore Gold.

RITA. You better had hit the deck.

TUSH. Okay. But please sleep on it. Sweet dreams, angel.

TUSH goes.

MAY notices that MORDY has dropped off to sleep.

MAY. Looks like someone's taken his advice.

She shakes MORDY slightly.

Wakey-wakey, Wee Willy Winky.

MORDY stirs.

MORDY. May?

MAY. There's a bed made up in the shrapnel room for you.

MORDY. A bed?

MAY. Better than a chair. Even if the window's boarded.

MORDY. What about you?

MAY. I can share with Gertie and Rita.

MORDY. What about snuggles with your hubby tonight?

RITA. She's exhausted, Mordy.

MORDY. . . . Oh, I love you, May . . . I love you more than life itself . . .

> (*Singing*.) My Bonnie lies over the ocean
> My Bonnie lies over the sea . . .

MAY. Oh Mordy, please. Stop it.

MORDY. My Bonnie lies over the ocean . . .

MAY. Mordy!

MORDY. Oh, bring back my Bonnie to me . . .

MAY. That's enough.

MORDY. Bring back! Bring back! . . .

MAY. Mordy! Stop it!

RITA. Shh, May.

MAY. Well, if we must talk about bringing back, what about our Arnold? If anyone's gone AWOL then it's him.

RITA. Hush now, May.

MAY. No, I bloody well won't hush.

MORDY. F-minus, May Fischer, for swearing . . .

MAY. I'll swear all I bloody bloody well like. What right has he to remortgage the house without asking us? It isn't his. It belongs to Rita, me and Gertie as much as it does to him.

MORDY. Do you want for anything, my love? Don't I provide you with a comfortable life?

MAY. There is smashed glass all over the living room.

MORDY. We'll fix all the windows at home in no time. Everything will soon be back to normal.

Silence.

MAY. Gertie has made up the bed nicely in the shrapnel room for you, Mordy.

MORDY *kisses* MAY *on her head.*

MORDY. Don't stay up too late, little pickle.

MAY. Night night.

RITA. Night night, Mordy.

MORDY. Night night.

MORDY *goes.*

RITA. I wish that Arnold had never got married.

MAY. It's our fault entirely. We shouldn't have let him make such a stupid mistake.

RITA. It's worse than a mistake. It's a disaster. I can't believe what she's done to him. He doesn't draw any more. He plays the violin less and less because she moans about the racket.

MAY. It would break Daddy's heart. It breaks my poor heart to see him so fat and sweaty and keeping accounts for his father-in-law. A butcher, for God's sake! And recording the minutes for the council? Being doled out instructions by Peter O'Donnell who lords it over him . . . like a preening cock . . . Him and his car rides . . . Can't Arnold see what's going on?

GERTIE *enters.*

RITA. I can't take any more! I can't bear it!

GERTIE. Oh sweetheart, what's the matter?

RITA. Why did Arnold let her take my bedroom off me?

GERTIE. You'll get it back soon. We'll have to speak to him . . .

RITA. I won't ever get it back. It's been invaded. I should never have moved out. I should have put up a fight. That was my bedroom. This is meant to be our home. And didn't we win the war? Where's the good life we were promised? I want to go home to New York and be happy and find true love and taste kasha knishes. But it seems further away than ever. Where has it all gone?

RITA *starts to sob.*

GERTIE. Oh darling, now I can't bear it. Please don't cry.

RITA*'s sobs increase in intensity.*

RITA. I'm not crying . . . I'm not . . . I'm not . . . I'm not . . .

She sobs and sobs.

GERTIE. Oh Rita, I want what's best for you. You do know that. And there is one sure-fire way for you to get to New York and live there in style.

GERTIE *gives* RITA *a hankie from her pocket.*

If you marry Tush you'll have more bedrooms than you can count. Alright, so he's no oil painting out of uniform. But you can even live on the Upper West Side again. And he adores you. You'll want for nothing. Think about it.

RITA. But I don't want to live in style with lots of bedrooms.

GERTIE. Isn't this what you're really so upset about? Having to share with me like a pair of old spinsters?

RITA. I'm upset because . . . because . . . I work so hard for such long hours doing meaningless office jobs . . . for no real purpose . . . I'm upset because my life still amounts to nothing . . . I'm upset because nowhere in the world is safe for us . . . I'm upset because I just don't know where I belong . . . Where do I belong?

GERTIE. With Tush, sweetheart.

RITA. But he isn't planning to go back to New York . . . He's going to settle in Palestine . . .

GERTIE. That won't last long. Believe me.

MAY. Believe her.

RITA. Why do you never take anyone seriously who believes in a cause?

GERTIE. Idealists always come down to earth with a bump, darling. Especially Tush.

MAY. They'll hand him a shovel when he reaches the kibbutz, and he'll be on the next boat back to New York before they begin Hava Nagillah.

RITA. But that's the only thing I find attractive about him, his idealism.

GERTIE. Well, that's more than enough. I'd settle for someone old and ugly if he was as decent as Tush.

RITA. But do I have it in me to give my whole life? Sometimes I feel I do . . . But then . . . But then . . .

GERTIE. He's devoted to you.

MAY. A man's devotion is never enough. Unless it matches your devotion for him. Believe me, Rita. Don't make the mistake I did.

GERTIE. Believe me, it'd be a bigger mistake to let him go.

DEBBIE *enters with a very old and battered suitcase. She smiles politely and places it to the side of the room.*

The three sisters all look at the case.

DEBBIE *smiles again and exits.*

What on earth is she doing with Beil's old case!

MAY. Oh aye, perhaps Her Royal Highness is about to jump ship at last with her Irish vagabond. Hallelujah.

GERTIE. Stop being so facetious.

MAY. You'd be even happier to see the back of her than I would. Admit it, Gertrude Lasky.

GERTIE. I'm not admitting anything so callous, you wicked creature.

MAY. Look at her, Rita, she can barely contain a smile.

GERTIE. Do I look like I'm smiling?

RITA. Watch it, Gertie, or your face'll crack.

GERTIE. Stop ganging up on me.

MAY and RITA *mock* DEBBIE, *singing about the 'Debbie-witch to 'Ding-Dong! The Witch is Dead', from* The Wizard of Oz.

Shush! She'll hear you.

MAY and RITA *sing louder.* GERTIE *tries to cover their mouths with her hands. She can't help but start to laugh with exhaustion, a release.*

Shush! Shush!

The three sisters laugh and sing together that 'The Debbie-witch has fled'.

MAY. Now listen to me. I have something to tell you. It's important.

GERTIE. This is really not the time.

MAY. I can't keep it to myself any longer.

GERTIE. You better had, May. Believe me.

MAY. And believe me, I am bursting at the seams.

GERTIE. Honestly. At your age. Be sensible.

MAY. But I've fallen in love. Totally in love. I didn't ask for it or expect it but it's happened. And, oh my God . . . it's wonderful.

GERTIE. That's enough. More than enough.

MAY. But I've only just begun. I could pack my suitcase tomorrow, and I will given half the chance. He's the only man in the world for me . . . Can't you see?

Silence.

It's Vince.

GERTIE. Stuff and nonsense.

MAY. I'm not letting go of the man I love. We'll find a way to be together. Damn it, I can sell up my share of this house. Then he and I will find a place of our own where we can rescue his girls from their crazy mother and I can make up for everything they've never had.

GERTIE. Listen to yourself! You don't even like children.

MAY. I know that this doesn't sound like cynical old May. But love fills you with such fire . . . such hope . . . Anything can come true.

Silence.

Gertie, you'll look after Mordy once I've gone, won't you?

Silence.

Make him happy.

Silence.

We'll all be so much happier this way. The way it should have been.

ARNOLD *enters. He heads for the case and picks it up.*

ARNOLD. Better put this somewhere safe for Auntie B. But please don't tell Debbie I've taken it.

He heads out and then suddenly remembers something.

Oh Gertie, I've been wondering about the Hogarth print in the study. That must be worth something, surely . . .

GERTIE. Not now, Arnold.

Silence.

ARNOLD. What?

Silence.

ARNOLD *wheezes mildly.*

What have you all got against me?

MAY. What on earth is happening to you?

ARNOLD. I don't know what you mean.

MAY. Arnold? This is May here. Your sister. Wakey-wakey. You'd better listen to me now and listen hard . . .

VINCE*'s voice can be heard just outside la-la-ing 'Let's Face the Music and Dance'.*

Oh God, I have a terrible feeling that I've forgotten to switch off the . . . downstairs . . . you know . . . the whatsit . . . the whojamaflip . . . Must see to it right away . . .

MAY *heads for the door.*

VINCE*'s refrain continues.*

ARNOLD. Where the hell are you going?

MAY. Tomorrow. We'll talk about this tomorrow. I mean it, Arnold. Sleep well, my darlings.

MAY *rushes off.*

GERTIE. For once I agree with May. Let's get to bed.

ARNOLD. Let's get a few things straight first.

GERTIE. Oh Arnold . . .

ARNOLD. Please show some respect. Even if it's only for a minute.

RITA. Oh Arnold . . .

ARNOLD. Oh Gertie. Oh Rita.

MORDY *enters.*

MORDY. May?

Silence.

MORDY *wanders out.*

ARNOLD. Please, the pair of you. Hear me out. Please. A little respect. That's all. And for my wife too. You've had it in for her from the very first and I've had enough of it. Debbie is a gem. I'm lucky to have such a loving and sweet and devoted wife. Take those looks of disbelief off your faces. She's a natural mother, so caring and considerate. No man could ask for more . . . No man could want for better . . . Some respect, please. And for my work also. I am proud to be of some real use in the reconstruction of our city and to help my father-in-law run a successful and expanding business. And all those committees need a man like me. Especially the appeal for the home for aged Jews. I can't think of a better reason to put my PhD aside for the time being. Scholarship hardly pays the bills . . .

GERTIE. But, Daddy . . .

ARNOLD*'s wheezing deepens.*

ARNOLD. I haven't finished. I have something else to say. It's about the house. I need some capital . . . So I've had to re-mortgage. And as for Daddy, if he'd left me a trust fund like he left you girls . . .

GERTIE. Trust fund, for heaven's sakes . . .

ARNOLD. . . . then maybe I wouldn't have to eat into my equity. But there it is.

MORDY *enters again.*

MORDY. I seem to have lost her completely.

Silence.

MORDY *disappears.*

ARNOLD. So there you have it. And I'll thank you to show me some appreciation. You may not credit it, but I am trying to

do my best. And it's not necessarily all that easy. Not with all
the demands and not with . . . another baby on the way . . .
Which I wasn't expecting . . . not at all . . . Oh God . . .
What's happening to us? . . . This isn't how it's meant to be
. . . Oh Gertie. Oh Rita. Oh God, help me . . . Don't listen.
Don't believe a word I'm saying.

ARNOLD *goes out.*

RITA. Gertie.

Silence.

We just cannot live this way any more.

GERTIE. We have each other. We'll always have each other.

RITA. I have to make a new life. I'll say yes to Tush. There's
nothing else.

ACT FOUR

Monday, 5th July, 1948.

First thing in the morning.

RITA, NATE *and* TUSH *sit at the table, cluttered with piles of letters and newspapers, eating toast and drinking cups of tea.*

Their meal goes on in silence for a little while.

NATE*'s tea may well be fortified with something stronger. He is reading the newspaper which declares on the front page the launch of the National Health Service.*

TUSH *is reading a modern Hebrew phrase book.*

NATE. You do realise, I hope, that the introduction of this state medical service is simply part of a plot to convert Great Britain into a National Socialist economy. Little Stalins everywhere. Bunch of fascists.

Silence.

Tea drinking.

Is there no end to all this 'nationalisation'? Before we know it, the bloody trains will be running on time.

Silence.

And they're threatening to nationalise the gas now. Need I say any more?

RITA. Who wants the last piece of toast?

TUSH. 'Bread' is '*lechem*'. Not sure what 'toast' is. '*Ha*' is 'the'. You have '*Ha'lechem*', Rita.

RITA. Uncle Nate?

NATE. Enough toast for me, my dear. It can only be for you.

RITA. Don't mind if I do. *Todah rabbah.*

TUSH *nods with approval.*

NATE. Well, we doctors did try. We made our stand against this NHS thing. It's tyranny, I say. State tyranny parading as a social service . . . What do they think a doctor is? A bloody civil servant? . . . Telling you how to practise . . . But what do you two care? Off to where the sun for ever shines . . . And – what is it they say? – the rivers of milk and honey never curdle . . .

He raises a cup of tea.

To the bold pioneers! Spread your wings. Make haste away from the bombed-out remains of the most godforsaken city in this once great land that is fast flowing down the plughole. Cheers.

RITA. Oh Uncle Nate.

NATE *sighs.*

A knock on the door.

MORDY (*offstage*). Knockety-knock.

MORDY *enters, properly attired as deputy headmaster for a day at school. He now sports a moustache that looks very like that of Clement Attlee, bushy above his top lip.*

I had to pop by before school starts to wish you both all the best, all the very best.

RITA. Isn't May with you?

MORDY. She was barely up when I left. But she'll be along soon. She's determined to catch you before you disappear on us for ever.

RITA. Not for ever . . .

TUSH *grabs* MORDY*'s hand.*

TUSH. Goodbye then, Mordy . . . We will see each other again, I'm sure . . .

MORDY. By that time you two will be so bronzed and I'll be so grey that we'll hardly recognise each other.

MORDY grips TUSH's hand tight, and shakes and shakes.

You will be missed, greatly missed, my dear friend. I say friend, well, you're almost family . . .

RITA fiddles with a very modest engagement ring on her left hand.

TUSH. And I'll miss you, Mordy.

The handshake continues. MORDY can't quite let go.

I'll miss the rain and the park and the pier head . . .

RITA. You hardly ever go down there.

TUSH. I'll still miss it. And the crumpets at the Lyons' tea house and fish and chips from Yaffey's. I'll miss Mindy Solomons with elephantitis who plays a mean hand of gin rummy . . .

NATE plays an imaginary, sentimental violin.

. . . and not finding a seat at Greenbank shul on Yom Kippur and sneaking pork scratchings before the fast is out and a pint of Guinness at The Philharmonic pub . . .

NATE. My heart bleeds.

MORDY looks at his watch.

MORDY. Is there anything I can help you with before I have to get off?

RITA. What about the trunk on the first-floor landing?

TUSH. Could you give me a hand with that?

MORDY. Yes. Of course. Yes.

TUSH heads out of the room, followed by MORDY.

RITA. We're all flooding away in one big wave.

NATE. Ah, I once had a yen to brave the descent to London. The cafés of Soho, the racing dogs of Walthamstow, the quiet streets of St John's Wood. One day. Perhaps. Who knows?

RITA. You do need to move on somehow. I mean it.

NATE. Someone's got to be here if you decide to come back.

RITA. But, Uncle Nate . . .

NATE. You never know, munchkin. You never know . . .

RITA. Oh Uncle Nate . . .

NATE. No. I'm not going anywhere. One of us has to make a stand.

RITA. Then you must at least start by paying the rent . . . Straight away . . . You've got to keep her happy . . .

NATE. Well then, I will clean up my act and become the perfect, quiet, well-behaved and most kindly Great Uncle . . . That should calm her down . . .

NATE takes his key out of his pocket.

I still have my key. See.

He puts it into his top pocket, by his heart, and pats it safe. He sings a couple of lines from Sir Henry Bishop's 'Home! Sweet Home!'.

ARNOLD bustles in carrying a baby's bottle of milk. He shakes a drop onto the back of his hand then licks it off.

ARNOLD. 'Scuse me.

He leans across RITA and takes a muslin hanging over the back of the chair beside her. Then he bustles out with the faintest flicker of a wheeze.

MORDY and TUSH re-enter.

TUSH. . . . It's no big deal, Mordy. It's fine.

MORDY. Solly's a very queer egg at the best of times . . .

RITA. What's no big deal?

TUSH. We just happened to meet last night at The Grapes . . .

MORDY. A little birdie told me that words were exchanged and they were heated . . .

NATE. It was the Irish malt speaking.

MORDY. I gather that it rather got beyond words . . .

TUSH. Ach, do me a favour . . . There's more important things in life . . .

TUSH makes an irritated exit.

NATE. Pair of silly billies. Load of nonsense.

RITA. Why can't they just get on like they used to?

MORDY. In many ways, I suppose, it's a compliment, Rita. Two strapping fellows working themselves up into a lather over you.

RITA. I didn't ask them to, you know.

MORDY. Oh, the power of a lovely woman. As indeed you are, Rita. So very lovely. A bit like your sister. You both tend to get rather wrapped up in your own thoughts. Only you have a sweeter, truer nature. Not that May doesn't have an adorable nature too . . . Oh, everyone knows how much I adore her.

A loud thud in the hallway. RITA jumps.

DEBBIE (*offstage*). Which idiot put that trunk there! Arnold!

RITA. By this time tomorrow we should be arriving at the farm. I'll be in Kent. Me. Starting training for kibbutz life. This time next week I'll be hauling hay or milking the cows or feeding the chickens.

She runs back behind them, all the way to the windows and looks out onto the street.

Oh, they should be here soon to pick us up.

MORDY. Well, I'm very happy for you if this is what you really want.

NATE. I feel like a withered old ostrich stuck in the sand while all the little hummingbirds fly south. Spread your wings, my sparrows. Fan those feathers.

MORDY. Today seems to be the day for it. Quite a mass migration. And I don't care what they say, May is the best. I'm a lucky man, no matter what. I look around me. I see people like Herbie Wiener whose mother – God rest her soul – made him leave school at fourteen to go into the business. And now he's gone kaput. Had to close down the bakery. And he's no fool, is Herbie. And he needn't be in such a pickle. Whilst yours truly is deputy headmaster and happy for it, an educated man, and you can't ask for more than a decent education. You can make sense of life with an education. Not that you can't be top of the class and miserable . . . But I'm happy as Larry . . .

RITA *taps out half a scale on the piano.*

RITA. I won't hear these keys play any more . . . Nor will I have to watch Peter O'Donnell sitting down at table with his 'just-a-quick-cuppa, love' and secret 'bikky' from Debbie's stash . . .

MORDY. No sign of our deputy headmistress yet this morning?

RITA. Oh, she's coming. It doesn't take so long from Southport. And she has to be back at the grammar school for the afternoon.

MORDY. I do tell her to stop burning the midnight oil. But Gertie and I are as bad as each other. Where on earth is she?

MORDY *leaves.*

RITA. The bedroom seems hollow without her. The whole house does. So it's not so hard to leave. And New York's a distant memory now too. And Tush is such a mensch. I do feel somehow safe with him. But Israel's the place for us. Nowhere else. Not on this earth.

MAY *wanders into the drawing room and hovers beside the piano with* RITA, *who plays some more fragments of a scale.*

And we'll just have a little wedding. No fuss.

MAY. How romantic. To be married in a war zone.

RITA. Maybe not for you.

MAY *sighs.*

A wedding outdoors, he promises. At dusk. And by the time he smashes the glass and they all cheer '*Mazel tov*', it'll be dark. And we'll gather round the campfire with our chevreh and sing and dance . . .

MAY. I hope you'll think of us for at least a couple of seconds.

RITA. Oh May. Of course. You know how much I wish you and the others were coming too.

MAY. I still don't understand why you couldn't have got married here.

RITA. A new start in our new state.

MAY. If you're happy then I am.

RITA. I'm so excited I could burst. I was being so stupid this morning before breakfast . . . Getting all worked up . . . I really don't know what that was all about . . .

MAY. Oh Rita . . .

NATE. Silly sausage.

Sounds of voices in the hallway.

MORDY (*offstage*). Here they are!

DEBBIE (*offstage*). Gertie! Beil! Welcome to our humble abode.

RITA *goes out to the hallway.*

More sounds of GERTIE *and* BEIL *greeting and being greeted.*

NATE *immerses himself in his newspaper.*

MAY *joins him at the remains of the breakfast table.*

MAY. Lying low, are we?

NATE. Is it a crime?

MAY. Feeling sorry for ourselves?

NATE. Don't see why.

MAY. Hmmm.

NATE. Hmm yourself.

Silence.

MAY. Can I ask you something?

NATE. Sounds ominous.

MAY. How much did you love Mummy?

NATE. Oh Esty . . .

Silence.

More than words can say.

MAY. And did she return the favour?

NATE. That I can't quite recall.

The door opens. Crying child in the hallway.

ARNOLD *dashes in and picks up a teddy bear from one of the drawing-room chairs. He also grabs the spinning top from Act One. Then he dashes out.*

MAY. Has my one-and-only dropped by yet?

NATE. Not that I know.

MAY. It doesn't work, you know, pretending that nothing very serious is happening. Because it is happening. And it is serious. — Stay CS

Silence.

I never wanted to be hard as nails, Uncle Nate. But whenever I try to seize at big, bold life with both hands, it has this awful way of shrinking down to size. I can vaguely remember marvelling at Mordy in his crisp white shirts. And now all I see are the rings around the collar. Daddy was right. I should have kept my hands off. Poor Gertie. I am a rotten sister. But there is a heart in here somewhere. Even if it does have 'disappointment' written through the middle like a stick of Blackpool rock. It's no good trying to grab at happiness. It doesn't bloody work. And it never will. And look at him. Our one and only Arnold. Where's it all gone? Poof! Up the chimney. All our hopes and dreams. All his talent. All that money spent on his fine education. Poof! Poof! Poof!

Sounds of a child and baby crying in the hallway and up the stairs.

Child screaming.

Shushes and cajolings from DEBBIE *and* GERTIE.

The crying recedes.

ARNOLD *enters with teddy bear.*

ARNOLD. Teddy no good. Bobby wants his schmutty.

NATE. Don't we all?

ARNOLD. You haven't seen it have you? The little blue blanket.

NATE. That filthy rag on the stair? Flushed it down the lav.

ARNOLD *looks aghast.*

MAY *laughs.*

NATE *laughs.*

ARNOLD *shakes his head warningly at* NATE.

NATE *looks at his watch.*

Flight of the bumblebees should be completed by the hour of lunch. Lucky blighters, the lot of them.

Silence.

ARNOLD. Did something untoward happen yesterday evening at The Grapes?

NATE. It was nothing. Tush and I were merely taking a little farewell crawl around the public houses of this sodden city when we happened upon the errant Solomon Salzburger brooding away in a dark corner and gripping in his perfumed paw some tome on Being Nothing or Nothing Being or somesuch by that French thingumajiggy . . .

MAY *and* ARNOLD. Jean-Paul Sartre.

NATE. So Tush did the chummy thing and offered the soldier a pint. For old times' sake. And two, or maybe four, jars later the conversation gets a little overheated. And boys being boys, there's a bit of shoving and pushing until Solly trips and knocks himself on the side of the bar. He blames Tush, erupts like a volcano, spits a lot of vicious bile about our Rita's blackened virtue – very medieval – then he smashes his glass and would have gone for him had the landlord not intervened. And to cap it all, Sol then goes and challenges Tush to some kind of bare-knuckle duel . . .

NATE *pulls out his little notebook.*

I'm taking bets. My money's on Sol. Three-to-four favourite.

MAY. Tush is keeping well away, I hope.

NATE. You hope in vain.

MAY. Are you joking?

NATE. When would I ever joke about a face-to-face slug-out?

ARNOLD. But this sounds like it's really getting out of hand . . .

MAY. Nate Weinberg! You should have nipped this in the bud never mind whipping it up.

NATE. Storm in a teacup. Let them see it through. Then they can kiss and make up. And cuddle on the verandah at dusk.

MAY. Does Tush even know how to bare-knuckle fight?

NATE. Maybe we should make Solly ten-to-four favourite. Are you in, Arnold?

ARNOLD. Not if it's illegal.

NATE. What does the law matter in affairs of the heart. Eh, May? What does any of it matter?

MAY. Words, words, words . . . Has it started to rain yet? . . . Oh my God, look! The sun's still shining. I'm going into the garden. I've got a headache. Tell Vince where I am . . . He should be here soon . . . Whether the weather be cold . . . Whether the weather be hot . . .

MAY *exits into the garden*.

ARNOLD *looks the teddy in the eye*.

ARNOLD. Well, Mr Teddy, looks like you and me are going to be the only sane ones left.

(*Puts on a teddy voice*.) 'Oh dear, Arnold, is everyone going off and leaving you behind?'

(*In his own voice*.) I'm afraid they are, Ted. I'm afraid they are.

NATE. Funny thing, fatherhood. Nearly as funny as marriage.

ARNOLD (*puts on teddy voice*). 'Oh Great Uncle Nate, why did you never get married to a sweet and loving and adorable wife like lucky Arnold did?'

NATE. No comment.

ARNOLD *drops teddy unceremoniously onto the table*.

ARNOLD. You know, sometimes Debbie reminds me of an overstuffed teddy bear . . . with a sawdust brain and hidden claws in her vicious little paws . . . Don't say I said anything.

NATE. Schtum's the word.

ARNOLD. Or she's a clockwork mouse that scurries mindlessly in circles driving you crazy . . . And you have trouble working out why you used to love it to bits . . . and could

never bear to stop playing with it . . . but can't even face the
thought of it any more . . .

NATE. Tell you what, my lad, it might be too late for me, but
you've still got some life left in you. Run for the hills, man.
Leg it out of here like your sisters, before you turn into a
teddy too. Or, God forbid, a schmutty.

The door opens ominously as if all by itself.

Silence.

SOLLY *walks in like a predator on the prowl.*

SOLLY. For a man to be what he is, he must learn what he is
not. Nate, it's nearly time.

NATE. Righty-o.

SOLLY. Time to show Romeo how it is and is not.

NATE. Is that right?

SOLLY. Don't worry. I'll just knock him into shape.

NATE. Who said that I was worried?

SOLLY *and* NATE *make a purposeful exit.*

Voices in the hallway.

RITA *enters.*

RITA. Arnold, Potty Potter's here for you with the papers. From
Joe Pollack.

ARNOLD. Ah right.

ARNOLD *doesn't move.*

RITA. He's waiting.

MORDY *enters.*

MORDY. Did someone say that May was in the garden?

MORDY *looks out towards the garden.*

May, my dear! May!

MORDY *goes out towards the garden.*

TUSH, *now wearing a kibbutznik hat, enters and brushes past* MORDY.

TUSH. Mordy seems to be in very good spirits today.

RITA. What did Solly just say to you by the front door?

TUSH. I didn't hear anything.

RITA. Then why have you gone so pale?

DEBBIE (*offstage*). Arnold!

ARNOLD. Alright!

ARNOLD *goes off into the hallway.*

TUSH. Say, Rita. I gotta go somewhere for a little while. Will you be okay?

RITA. Where?

TUSH. Say goodbye to a few guys . . . Ya know . . .

RITA. Like you did at The Grapes last night?

TUSH. I'll be less than an hour.

RITA. But Tush . . .

He puts his arm round her and kisses her warmly.

TUSH. It won't take long.

RITA. Promise?

TUSH. Sweetheart, I'll be back with you as soon as I can.

RITA. You better had be.

TUSH. Can you believe that we're actually beginning our whole new life together? We're making our dreams come true. It's incredible. I want to make you happier than you've ever been. I want you to love me as much as I love you.

RITA. Oh Teddy. You're my best friend. My tremendous chum. And we're comrades in arms, aren't we? I wish I knew what you mean about loving so much. I so want to feel that way too. But I never have. Not even halfway. Maybe I'm not even capable of it.

TUSH. I'm still searching for the way . . .

RITA. Oh, please don't . . .

TUSH. What else can I do? Tell me, honey.

RITA. Just let things be as they are.

TUSH. A clue. Give me a tiny hint? What else can I do?

RITA. How do I know?

Silence.

TUSH. So, I'll just say shalom. Peace be with you, my Rita, and I'll see you again very soon. Your passport and tickets are on the piano. See. Don't forget them.

RITA. I'm coming too.

TUSH. No you're not.

Silence.

Say, Rita.

RITA. Yes?

TUSH. You couldn't find me a book to read for the train journey, could ya? You got so many to choose from here. Be a pal. Make it light.

RITA. See you soon.

TUSH *gives her a big kiss and makes a hasty exit.*

TUSH. *Lehitraot.* See ya.

RITA *almost follows* TUSH *and then checks herself. She descends into deep reflection and wanders over to the piano, where she sits staring at the keys in silence. Then she leans her head against the piano and closes her eyes.*

ARNOLD *hovers in the doorway.* DEBBIE *is on his heels.*

DEBBIE. Don't keep Daddy waiting any longer, Arnold.

ARNOLD. I need to read them thoroughly first.

DEBBIE. Then get on with it.

DEBBIE *vanishes.*

ARNOLD *enters, carrying a thick wad of papers.*

ARNOLD. Honestly.

ARNOLD *sits at the table and stares at the papers blankly.*

RITA *gets up and leaves.*

Well, Daddy, are you watching this?

He picks up a pen from the table.

When did you and Mummy first take over from the Wein-
bergs and move in here? Before the Great War. Before the
four of us existed. And now you're a grandpa, so I'm sure
you'll understand that our Bobby and baby Marilyn must
be well taken care of. That's the only reason I'm doing this,
Daddy. And Joe Pollack is family. A more doting grandpa
you couldn't hope to find. And the mortgage is weighty. I
don't suppose that this is quite what you hoped for me. To
be bought out. Or to sell out. Depends how you look at it.
But then not much ends up how we expect, does it, Daddy,
when you're stuck in a community of, what, ten thousand
Jews, that seems like it's about fifty thousand strong. God
help me. Small-minded busybodies always poking their
nose in, giving advice, expecting you to fit in and not stand
out. And all they care about isn't learning and books and
the meaning of life or the beauty of art, but what they eat
and what's scarce and endless bloody weather and could
they one day afford their own car or even a television, now
wouldn't that be something? And they enjoy a few drinks
and cigarettes, if they can get hold of any these days, and a
good gossip and a right old kvetch and bit of rumpy-pumpy
behind the hubby's back and a new hat for yom tov and on

and on and on it goes, and this is what they teach the kids
whose spark of life is snuffed out just like theirs so that
they carry on being the same small-minded, tunnel-
visioned, self-important, interfering busybodies going
nowhere for ever!

He looks through the papers sadly.

Oh Gertie. Oh Rita. Dearie, dearie me. Oh May.

DEBBIE*'s voice in the hallway. And* POTTER*'s.*

DEBBIE (*offstage*). 'Hello, Mr Potter,' says Marilyn. 'Do you
like my pink and red dress that Granny Pollack saved all her
coupons for?'

POTTER (*offstage*). She's nearly as pretty as her mother.

DEBBIE (*offstage*). And ten times as mouthy when she wants
to be.

DEBBIE *laughs.*

POTTER (*offstage*). Nothing wrong with a woman who speaks
her mind, Mrs L.

DEBBIE (*offstage*). Well, I'm glad that someone round here
appreciates a bit of oomph.

DEBBIE *enters, pushing a pram that she settles right next
to* ARNOLD.

Have you still not signed those deeds?

ARNOLD. Give a man a chance.

DEBBIE. You've already been through them with a nit comb.
There's nothing else to pick over.

ARNOLD *slowly begins to unscrew the lid of his fountain pen.*

Get on with it.

DEBBIE *stands over* ARNOLD *whilst he signs.*

Don't keep Mr Potter waiting any longer.

ARNOLD *screws the lid back onto his pen, takes up the deeds and walks slowly out of the room.*

DEBBIE *coos into pram.*

Who's your mummy, Marilyn? Who's your mummy then? Yes, you know who your mummy is, don't you? Yes you do.

Sudden and very raucous hooting and shouting from the street. An accordion plays a pioneer song. Voices sing in Hebrew.

RITA *comes back in.*

Rita, sounds like your lift's here.

RITA. Is Tush back?

DEBBIE. His case is still filling the hallway.

RITA. They're early.

More hooting.

DEBBIE. Will you please go out there and tell your friends to be quiet. They're showing us all up with their bloomin' hora songs.

RITA. I'll take them into the garden until Tush is back . . .

DEBBIE. Just tell them to come back a bit later, if you don't mind, Rita . . . And to lower the volume, please. They'll frighten the children, the din they're making.

RITA *rushes out.*

DEBBIE *returns to the pram.*

What a funny noise, isn't it, Mini Moo Moo? What are the silly people doing out there? What are they making all the hoo-hah for?

The hooting dies down a little. As does the singing.

GERTIE *enters, followed by* BEIL.

GERTIE. I don't know where those Habonim people think they are. They're not in Israel yet. At least they could wait till they're on their farm.

DEBBIE. I couldn't agree more. Don't we agree with Auntie Gertie, Marilyn? Don't we agree with our very favourite auntie?

BEIL. But have you given them anything for the journey? I baked cakes. Did Rita get the marble cake, Gertie?

GERTIE. Rita got the marble cake, Beil.

BEIL. And the Victoria sandwich. Catering-size. They're going such a long way and there's quite a bunch of them. They need supplies. I was taking old Mrs Davies out on the sands on Saturday afternoon and I said that my niece was going halfway across the world and I might never see her again. She doesn't even bat an eyelid. Out come her coupons. 'Some people plant trees. I'll donate a few eggs.'

VINCE *enters*.

And the jam came from Mrs Max – if she's not at least ninety, then I'm twenty-one – so I do a bit of cleaning for her when her daughter can't come up from St Anne's. Everybody knows who I am. It's 'Beil, can you help us with this, help us with that, what a gem you are!' And Gertie tells me off for nochschlepping around for the old biddies . . .

GERTIE. This is meant to be your comfortable retirement, Auntie B . . .

BEIL. Don't I play a bit of bowls on a Wednesday afternoon?

DEBBIE. Oh, 'scuse us a mo, Beil, we'd best make sure our Bobby's a happy boy now. And we're so glad, Great Auntie, that you're settling down out of town. We always knew you would.

DEBBIE *makes a swift exit, with pram*.

BEIL. Thank the Lord above for out of town.

VINCE. Looks like you've found the perfect place.

BEIL. Well, I am. I have.

GERTIE. So unpack that old suitcase of yours.

BEIL. Well . . . as it happens . . . I've taken out the pair of shoes. They're in my bedroom dresser. They seem to like it there.

GERTIE. *Mazel tov!*

VINCE. Excuse me . . . but I need to get to the station soon for my train . . .

GERTIE. May is in the garden.

VINCE. Okay . . .

BEIL. Let me get her for you.

BEIL *exits*.

VINCE. I've gotten so used to this house, to you all. It's so familiar now.

GERTIE. Very familiar. Yes.

VINCE. One last look.

GERTIE. You make this sound terribly final.

VINCE. It is.

GERTIE. And what about your wife and daughters? Will they join you in Israel?

VINCE. To settle there? . . . We'll see . . . I dunno how it'll work out . . .

GERTIE. Oh, it will be strange not hearing the American accents around. I've grown so used to you too. I could pretend that I was already halfway to New York with our Yanks here.

VINCE. I can't find the words to thank you enough for your kindness and hospitality and . . . Gertie, please don't think ill of me . . . I'd hate there to be any bad feelings . . .

GERTIE. May should be here any minute . . .

VINCE. It's strange times, Gertie. The war filled up our lives, right? That was some big reason to keep going. And when it ended, there was dancing in the streets. Because we'd won. Because the long struggle seemed to be over. But, if I'm honest, war brings out the best in me. Peace is like a big hole. I can't find the point in it. I gotta head for the battle. Maybe one day things'll change . . . Peace suits you better, Gertie. You got a vocation. You got respect . . . It's different for May . . .

GERTIE. It's not easy for any of us.

MAY *enters*.

VINCE. I'm here to say goodbye.

MAY *runs to* VINCE *and embraces him*.

GERTIE *retreats into the drawing room*.

MAY. Ask me again what you asked me before.

VINCE. May, honey . . .

MAY. Ask me again.

Silence.

'How about coming with me, May?'

VINCE *says nothing*.

How about it, Vince?

VINCE *still says nothing*.

MAY *takes his face in her hands and kisses him passionately*.

GERTIE. May, please . . .

VINCE *pulls away*.

MAY *yelps with pain and starts to sob*.

VINCE. Oh sweetheart . . . honey . . . Come on now . . . I'll write you . . . You write me . . . We've talked about this . . . Please, May . . . Enough . . .

MAY sobs and sobs.

MORDY enters.

GERTIE. May, enough now!

MAY sobs even more hysterically.

VINCE. Darling . . .

GERTIE. Stop it!

Hooting of car horns and singing Hebrew songs outside.

MAY wails.

VINCE. It's time . . .

VINCE looks to GERTIE and sees MORDY.

Right. Okay. It's time.

More hooting of horns and singing from outside.

VINCE prizes MAY off him.

It's time, honey . . . I must . . . Here . . .

He hands MAY over to GERTIE.

Take her . . . I'm late . . .

He nods a hasty, respectful goodbye to GERTIE and MORDY. He goes.

MAY sobs uncontrollably.

MAY. What's happening? Why's this happening? . . . Why? . . . Why? . . . How can it happen? . . . How? . . . Tell me how? . . .

GERTIE. Shush now. Shush . . .

MAY. Mummy . . . Mummy . . . Why? . . . Daddy? . . . Daddy?

GERTIE. Stop now . . . Stop . . .

MORDY. Let her have a good bawl. Let her wail her head off if needs be.

MAY *wails*.

I'm still here. Your Mordy's not going anywhere. Everything will be like it was before. No hard feelings. No grudges. I promise.

MAY *howls*.

We can get back to normal now.

MAY *howls and howls*.

GERTIE. It's going to be alright.

MAY *starts to gulp and steady herself. The sobs decrease*.

There now.

MAY *struggles to find some control*.

MAY. Whether the weather be hot . . . Or cold? . . . Whether be not . . . Weather be hot . . . Weather be not not not . . . I'm going off my rocker . . .

GERTIE. Deep breaths, darling. Big breaths.

MAY *gulps and tries to breathe more steadily*.

MORDY. Has she stopped crying now?

MAY *breathes*.

GERTIE. She's calming down a bit.

MORDY. There's a good girl.

GERTIE. There we are.

Sounds of a child screaming and bawling from upstairs.

MAY *breathes a little more steadily*.

MORDY. A-plus, May. A-plus.

GERTIE *laughs gently*.

MAY *wails slightly and then calms herself again.*

MAY. Whether the weather be cold . . . Or whether the weather be hot . . . Like it or not . . .

GERTIE. That's better . . .

Child bawls from upstairs again.

DEBBIE (*offstage, from right upstairs*). Arnold!

RITA *enters.*

RITA. May, are you alright?

MORDY. She's alright.

GERTIE. What about going upstairs for a lie-down?

MAY. Lie down where? Whose bedroom is left?

MAY *lets out some more sobs. She swallows them hard.*

I'm never going to sleep in this house ever again.

Awkward, painful silence.

MORDY. Dr Raisman told a cracker at the kiddush on Saturday. A mother and her son are at the beach in Blackpool. He's playing in the water and she's standing on the shore watching. All of a sudden, a huge wave appears from nowhere and sweeps the boy away. Mama raises her hands to the heavens. She screams and cries, 'Lord, how could you? Haven't I been a doting mother? Haven't I kept a kosher home? Haven't I lit candles every Friday night? Haven't I given everything to do you proud!' A voice booms from the sky, 'Alright, alright!' Another huge wave appears out of nowhere. As the water recedes, the boy is standing there, smiling and splashing as if nothing had ever happened. The voice booms again. 'I have returned your beloved son. Are you satisfied?' And mama looks up to the sky and raises her hands, 'He had a hat.'

RITA *and* GERTIE *laugh.*

GERTIE. 'He had a hat.'

MAY *starts to cry again.*

MORDY. Surely I deserve a B-plus for effort, May.

GERTIE *and* RITA *laugh encouragingly.*

DEBBIE *enters. She sees* MAY*'s tear-stained face and slumped form.*

DEBBIE. Oh, has Vince gone? I wanted to say goodbye. Arnold was meant to be seeing to Bobby, but of course he made a pig's ear of things as usual. The little darling's so clingy today. He can't bear that his favourite auntie is deserting him. He just doesn't understand, poor sausage. And I've told him that he can have his very own playroom now. Well, to share with Marilyn. But he's the big boy. And, you know, he says he'd rather have his Auntie Rita than her bedroom to play in. Oh, for heaven's sakes, who's gone and made such a dreadful mess all over the piano?

RITA. That's just my passport and ticket. It'll be gone soon. Don't worry.

DEBBIE. Oh Rita, Rita.

DEBBIE *hugs* RITA.

Are you really wearing that dress for the train journey?

RITA. What's wrong with it?

DEBBIE. Oh, take no notice of me. I'm not trying to hurry you off. Quite the opposite. If you said that you wanted to stay another day, or week, or even month, then I'd be beside myself with joy. And it would cheer Bobby up no end. We'd all be delirious. But that stuff in your bedroom, are you planning to take it or is it for getting rid? And why are all these newspapers still here on the table! Where's Nate vanished off to now! If I've told him once about his stupid newspapers, I've told him a thousand times.

DEBBIE *picks up the newspapers. Underneath is a square of blue flannel, well-loved.*

Oh! Here it is! Right!

DEBBIE *picks up the newspapers and schmutty and storms out.*

MAY. That woman!

RITA. She's a human bulldozer.

MAY. She's an inhuman stormtrooper.

GERTIE. That's enough, May.

MAY. She's a one-person occupation force . . .

MORDY. She tries her best. We all try our best, sweetheart.

MAY. If only you'd all stop trying and just try stopping for once.

MORDY. Tell you what, I'll just leave you three girls to it for a few moments.

MORDY *slips away.*

Silence.

More hoots and singing from outside.

RITA. There's just the one car out there now. The others have gone ahead to Lime Street.

GERTIE. Better get a move on.

NATE *enters. His trousers and jacket are covered in brick dust.*

Nate, where on earth have you been?

NATE. Nowhere. It's nothing.

GERTIE. What's happened?

MAY. What?

NATE. A bit of a pickle . . . Load of nonsense . . . I've got a blistering bloody headache now . . .

MAY. Out with it, Nate.

GERTIE tries to help NATE off with his dirty jacket. He tries to hold it to him. She tugs. He lets it go. She removes it to reveal blood on his shirt. Saturated.

RITA gasps. MAY and GERTIE are struck dumb.

RITA. What's happened!

NATE. There's been a slug-out . . .

RITA. Go on.

NATE. . . . We agreed the rules . . . Clean fight . . . But . . . Solly . . . lost all control . . . And Tush . . . no chance . . . No chance at all . . .

RITA. I knew it.

Silence.

NATE. Have you seen my newspaper? . . . Not that it matters . . . Everything disappears round here . . .

RITA runs to NATE and clings to him. He stands stock-still like a lump of wood.

Insistent car horn from outside.

RITA. What do we do? . . . What do I do? . . . Uncle Nate? . . . Where shall I go now? . . . What do I do?

Silence.

RITA *clings.*

Now you needn't be so cross with me for planning to have my wedding so far away from you all in the desert.

NATE *stands stock-still.*

Shall I stay? . . . Do I still go without him? . . . I don't know what to do . . .

NATE *prizes RITA's arms from him.*

NATE. Well, that's the end of that dream too.

NATE's hands are shaking. He searches his jacket pockets. He has trouble getting his fingers into the top pocket. He withdraws the front-door key and places it on top of the piano not far from RITA's passport and ticket.

NATE *leaves*.

MAY. We must go on.

RITA. You're right. I must go out to the kibbutz. And devote my life to tending orange groves and patrolling the fences and throwing grenades. I'll be brave like I'm meant to be. Like Tush made me feel I could be. I can still be brave without him. We've been given a miracle in our lifetime. That's what Tush says. We mustn't waste it.

She is fighting the urge to cry.

I knew it would go wrong. I knew it. No. I'll go and I'll work. And I'll fight. I'll just do it. I won't worry whether there's another disaster around the corner. I'm just going to knuckle down. Even if it keeps going wrong. I'll knuckle down.

The accordion strikes up again outside, playing a pioneering song.

MAY. And there's no room at this inn any more.

MAY *gets the passport and ticket from the piano.*

Sounds of running down the stairs in the hallway.

DEBBIE (*offstage*). Arnold! Arnold!

MAY *gives the ticket and passport to* RITA.

MAY. Either we die. Or we live. That's all.

MAY *turns on the radio. It is playing an instrumental version of the Gershwins' 'Strike Up the Band'.*

RITA. Tomorrow. I'll go. I will. Tomorrow.

MAY *sings softly along to the radio.*

GERTIE. We're not done yet, sisters. We're only just beginning. This is a whole new era. The world is changing and there's everything riding on it. We've each got to play our part. So many opportunities lie before us. We mustn't waste them. Not much further to go. Remember that wartime spirit. Dig in those heels. Push those boulders up, up, up the mountain. Nearly there. And we'll see. We will see . . .

MORDY *enters pushing Marilyn's pram.*

ARNOLD *follows with a basket into which he starts to clear up the toys lying dotted around.*

MAY *and* GERTIE *sing the last verse and final, rousing chorus of 'Strike Up the Band'.*

The End.

Glossary

Alter kaker	senile old man
Bris	ritual of circumcision, removal of foreskin, of male baby
Chassidim	member of Jewish mystical movement founded in eighteenth-century Poland
Cheder	Hebrew school for religious instruction held on Sundays
Chevreh	band of friends and comrades
Eshet Chayil	woman of worth, a good wife
Goyshe	non-Jewish
Habonim	'The Builders', Zionist youth organisation
Hava Nagillah	traditional song
Havdallah	ceremony held on Saturday evening for celebrating end of Sabbath and start of new week
Herzl	Theodore Herzl, 1860–1904, Austro-Hungarian Jewish journalist, founder of modern political Zionism
Hora	circle folk dance
JNF tin	blue-and-white tin for collection of money for Jewish National Fund
Kasha	boiled or baked buckwheat
Kaffiyah	traditional Arab headdress, scarf and headband
Kibbutz	collective agricultural settlement
Kibbutznik hat	bucket-shaped cotton hat worn by workers on kibbutz

Kiddush	celebration of drinks and snack foods over which blessings are made, usually after Sabbath morning service in synagogue
Knish	Russsian Jewish baked or fried turnover filled with potato or meat or cheese
Kugel	baked potato pudding
Kvetch	good old moan
Latkes	fried potato cakes
Le'chayim	'to life', drinking toast
Lehitraot	'till we meet again' (modern Hebrew)
Mazel tov	'good luck', celebratory
Mensch	very decent fellow
Nochschlepper	one who does the chores
Nudnik	no-good, boring pest
Olev hashalom	'rest in peace'
Pesach	festival of Passover celebrating liberation from slavery in Egypt
Pogrom	mass slaughter of Jews by Cossacks
Schmaltz herring	fatty, pickled herring
Shabbos	Sabbath (on a Saturday)
Shiksa	non-Jewish woman
Shiur	lesson
Shtetl	small Jewish town or village in Pale of Settlement in Tsarist Russia
Shul	synagogue
Shyster	rip-off merchant
Siddur	daily prayer book
Todah rabbah	'thank you very much' (modern Hebrew)
Yahrzeit candle	memorial candle for the deceased
Yom Kippur	Day of Atonement, festival and fast
Yom tov	holy day and festival

A Nick Hern Book

Three Sisters on Hope Street first published in Great Britain in 2008 as a paperback original by Nick Hern Books Limited, 14 Larden Road, London W3 7ST, in association with Hampstead Theatre, London and the Liverpool Everyman and Playhouse

Three Sisters on Hope Street copyright © 2008 Diane Samuels and Tracy-Ann Oberman

Diane Samuels and Tracy-Ann Oberman have asserted their moral right to be identified as the authors of this work

The front cover image shows Liverpool in the 1940s
Title design: Uniform
Cover design: Ned Hoste, 2H

Typeset by Nick Hern Books, London
Printed in the UK by CPI Bookmarque, Croydon, CR0 4TD

A CIP catalogue record for this book is available from the British Library

ISBN 978 1 85459 576 8